black girl, no magic

Kimberly McIntosh is a writer and researcher. She has written for a range of publications including the *Guardian*, *The Washington Post*, the *Independent*, the *Metro* and *Vice*. Between 2016 and 2020, she was the dating columnist at *gal-dem*, an award-winning online magazine committed to sharing perspectives of people of colour. Kimberly has discussed her research on BBC Radio 4 and 5 Live, BBC News and Sky News. She is a trustee at *Wasafiri* magazine, a quarterly British literary magazine covering international contemporary writing. *black girl, no magic* is her first book.

black girl, no magic

essays and reflections on living whilst black

kimberly mcintosh

THE BOROUGH PRESS

The Borough Press
An imprint of HarperCollins*Publishers* Ltd
1 London Bridge Street
London SE1 9GF

www.harpercollins.co.uk

HarperCollins*Publishers*
Macken House,
39/40 Mayor Street Upper,
Dublin 1,
D01 C9W8

First published by HarperCollins*Publishers* 2023
1

A catalogue record for this book is available from the British Library

Hardback ISBN: 9780008477042
Trade Paperback ISBN: 9780008477059

Typeset in Minion Pro by Palimpsest Book Production Ltd,
Falkirk, Stirlingshire

Printed and bound in the UK using
100% Renewable Electricity by CPI Group (UK) Ltd

This book is produced from independently certified FSC™ paper to ensure
responsible forest management.

For more information visit: www.harpercollins.co.uk/green

For my mum, Jackie, for letting me choose my own path and trusting I would find my way home.

I was changing the way I dressed, the way I talked to people. Being the smartest I could be. Being the most articulate in the room. Changing people's perception on a daily basis. It was a lot of pressure. And then actually, you start to lose yourself.

Ashley Walters, *How to Fail with Elizabeth Day* podcast (2022)

So the voice that I now seek is both individual and collective, personal and political, one reflecting the intersection of my unique biography with the larger meaning of my historical times.

Patricia Hill Collins, *Black Sexual Politics* (2004)

black girl, no magic

Contents

Introduction

The second time it happened I was looking at a birthday cake. It'd happened once before but I can't remember the specifics of it.

It's the kind of disorientation I imagine toddlers feel all the time. One minute they're falling asleep face down in a bed, only to awake sitting up and staring at wispy clouds through the coned hood of their pushchair, transported somewhere else without their knowledge.

It was the summer of 2012 and I watched my friend's birthday cake approaching his parents' kitchen island. I could see the pool in the distance and time started collapsing in on itself. I didn't know how I'd ended up here. I didn't feel anchored in anything. The contours of my life hadn't followed the shape of others' and the unfairness of that fact unsettled and overwhelmed me, although only momentarily. The candles were blown out, we raised our glasses and I was shaken back into my reality again. These were my friends and this was my real life.

Since childhood, I've known that people are governed by different rules depending on who they are: where they are born, whether they are rich or poor, the colour of their skin. The oft-repeated phrase, 'You have to work twice as hard as white people,' the clarion call of immigrant parents, a descriptive comment, a demand and an instruction, is one of the earliest examples that I remember. But I misinterpreted that lesson.

I thought that hard work alone would be enough. I was a devout disciple of respectability politics – the belief that if a marginalised group presented themselves better – by speaking 'well', never breaking the law, pulling up their baggy trousers or behaving 'properly' in public – they would do better in life by proving their worth and humanity to those suspicious of them. I did well in school because I was special, I thought. I had been lucky of course, but I was a 'grafter'. I kept my head down, had the right accent, was quiet and deferential. I worked the obligatory twice as hard. This was my path to the salvation of social mobility. Black people simply needed to be more excellent and all our ills would evaporate.

When stripped of humanity, reduced to caricature and condensed into tropes so deep-rooted people reach for them unconsciously, pushing back with evidence that you're good makes sense. In the house of horrors that is public imagination, surrounded by unrecognisable reflections of the self, there's an almost compulsive desire to build new mirrors that accurately show the world, and ourselves, who we really are. If only the detractors could see that we're polite, kind and gracious, hard-working and humble, not heathen, they will see we're not so different after all. But while in some scenarios it can be a form of resistance, these ideas and aspirations become tools that we voluntarily take up and build a prison that bars us from living freely. As Elizabeth Uviebinené writes in *Slay in Your Lane: The Black Girl Bible*, 'always trying to be excellent can put an unnecessary pressure on us'.[1]

Conforming to societal expectations of a 'good' black person is not the work required. By the time I got to university, I'd started to see that. You can't magic your way into fair treatment or justice. Excelling won't end racism or sexism.

This is no sob story. Life has been kind to me, although not without challenge. This is not the case for a lot of other people who look like me. I'm interested in why that is.

The academic Tressie McMillan Cottom writes that her essays 'always begin, by interrogating why me and not my grandmother? Why now and not then?'[2] and that is my preoccupation too. What do the realities of my childhood and twenties tell us about British society, what it means to get up every day and try to exist as a black person, a black woman, an ethnic minority, a working-class person, a middle-class person, a young professional, a friend, a girlfriend, a one-night stand? And what compelled me to write the world's cringiest travel diary and Facebook posts in the 2010s?

With a tiny bit of distance, I can see more clearly how societal norms, the stories told about black people and women and, as a consequence, the stories we tell ourselves, have influenced my actions and my self-esteem. I spent my twenties parading pieces of my personal life online with little thought of the consequences. I carelessly plastered exposing anecdotes from the frontline of sex, dating and clubbing onto the internet, where my past mistakes and at times embarrassing revelations are immortalised and live in perpetuity. But I was just attempting to make sense of what was happening to me. That's why in this book, I've included excerpts from my life that I find awkward or cringe-inducing. The story of our lives, when carefully drawn, can create an outline of the structures that shaped us: the accident of birth or kindness from a stranger that gave us a leg-up, or the negative stereotype or lack of money that blocked us or forced us to choose from a limited number of paths. But, like a camera in portrait mode, when I tell personal stories, I become the focus and the background is blurred. The tale it tells is a partial one.

The late activist Ambalavaner Sivanandan said that for him, writing 'has always been a way of fighting, whether through political analysis or creative fiction,'[3] and I feel that way too. So throughout these essays, the anecdotes I share will often have research and analysis sandwiched between them so that it's digestible (hopefully) but still speaks to the systemic problems and privileges that made my life what it is, that have hindered and helped me as I tried to get an education, make friends and find work, and explains what this means for people whose position in society is different to mine.

What I'm not here to tell you is how to be an anti-racist ally or how to love me. This isn't an instruction manual on how to end racism or how to feel less lost or overwhelmed. But I have broken up the serious bits with some jokes and lighter fare, because life is hard and we all need a laugh!

Black people, and black women, are not a monolith, and I do not, and cannot, represent us all. There is no one way to live a life and that is as true for black people as it is for anyone. Taken together, these essays encourage us to live our lives the way that suits us best, to try and do the right thing, to think beyond ourselves, own our choices and learn from them, and know that we have nothing to prove to anyone but ourselves and the people we love.

1 Mental health memoirs: GP's office, South London

April 2017

GP: You put 'can't sleep' on the online form. What's been happening?

Me: Yeah, I can't sleep. I wake up in the night and then I'm just stuck awake – thinking over and over again. My moods are just . . . I don't know. I thought maybe it was my period, but I've gone on contraception and I still feel the same. I don't know what's wrong. I can't sleep. My eye has started twitching. I feel overwhelmed all the time, but I don't know by what. I've had much harder times in my life. I have a really good life. There's nothing wrong with it. I have all the important things. I just don't know why this is happening to me.

GP: I've been seeing more and more people coming in with the same thing. Young women, mostly. Definitely try and cut back on the caffeine and the drinking. And if the feeling doesn't go away, or it comes back, call this number. I'm afraid the waiting list is pretty long. They'll probably refer you to an online course initially.

2 Middle-class safari

Now there comes a black expedition to darkest Britain. In the footsteps of Stanley, in the tradition of The World About Us, *and in a take-off of both, a black man's expedition now journeys along the Liverpool–Leeds canal to find the centre of Britain. On the way the intrepid explorers do what travellers and television safaris always have: they examine the quaint customs of the natives, delve into their folklore and record for posterity an exotic but fast-vanishing culture.*[1]

Synopsis for the satirical BBC Two film, *The Black Safari* by Horace Ové (1972)

Rich people don't have to be interesting, Kim.

A friend (2019)

Broken stuff interests me, it always has. I've had a fascination with the fractures of British society since I was seven or eight years old (totally normal behaviour). After a visit to London, I wanted to know why the City of Westminster looked so different to the (now demolished) Elephant and Castle shopping centre two miles down the road, where Dad went to send money to Jamaica. The inside of the mall was tired from financial neglect but brought to life by the tenacity of its immigrant-run businesses. Yet everything on the tourist trail, the London of looping open-top bus tours, the London of postcards, the Houses of Parliament and Portobello Road, shimmered with investment. I didn't know the name for those fractures or why they existed. But I felt their sharp edges and have spent my life trying to piece together the fragments – like a puzzle – understanding what I now know to call class and inequality.

In the mid-nineties the decisions of five people altered the course of my life.* I was caught in their compassionate crosshairs and transported from the working class to the environs of the upper-middle class. I was given a scholarship to a private school and, ever since then, I've wanted to know why I grew up poor while my friends were rich. Or at least retrospectively, that's what it feels like. I noticed that my peers and their families feared and judged not just certain people,** but certain places and things, and I wanted to know why. I wanted to know why some people thought it was completely ordinary to roast a whole chicken at random, just because they felt like it, not because it was Sunday or Christmas. And what was up with all the horses?

I say with no sense of shame that we were poor. I lived with my mother who worked as a part-time van driver. It is hard to work full time when you're responsible for school pick-up and drop-off. It's what, during my time as a social policy researcher, I'd call a persistent low income. Poverty isn't a permanent state, you undulate above and below its line. You are rarely far from its precipice and all it takes is an unexpected external event to push

* Back in the nineties, the headmistress of my school wanted to set up links with some black-led organisations. The then-Chair of The Runnymede Trust, a race-and-inequality-focused think-tank suggested reaching out to a Saturday School run by the African-Caribbean community. I happened to attend it every Saturday and had been earmarked as 'bright' by a staff member. It was 1998. New Labour had won a landslide election the year before. Talk of equal opportunity decked the halls of Westminster. Everything was going to be different. So, at the age of seven, I got a scholarship to a private prep school.

** Poor people, particularly anyone who wore sportswear as daywear before 2010.

you over the edge. You don't make enough to save up for rainy days. So when someone smashed the small, triangular window at the back of our car, we had to tape a plastic bag over it until we could afford to get it replaced. On school pick-up and drop-off, Mum would have to keep the engine running because there was no guarantee the car would start again. If you drove too fast the bag would loosen at the edges and flap frantically like the trapped wings of a bird trying and failing to fly. But you'd count yourself lucky because at least you had a car, others had it worse. If you weren't expecting a visitor you wouldn't answer the knock on the door. You speak in the lexicon of low income: overdrafts, Budgeting Loans, Tax Credits (now Budgeting Advances and Universal Credit) and topping up the gas and electric at PayPoint. It's a language sometimes alien to the middle class but that millions of people are fluent in. We lived in a mid-rise tower block where you hoped the piss in the lift was from a dog and not a person, although you could never know for sure. If you were smart, you used a key to press the buttons.

But it doesn't resemble the poverty porn of television docu-series either. I had a joyful childhood. Some years were more prosperous than others. A large family network meant you could club together and help each other out. My dad used to say that in Jamaica if you're poor, you're poor and everyone knows it. In England, you can hide, especially after Primark and Makro opened in town.

My parents had divorced and my dad remarried, leaving not only a financial gap that child support alone couldn't really make up for, but the cultural capital he carried left with him too. He is from a middle-class family in Jamaica, went to boarding school there, and has a master's degree. My mum grew up with my gran and her four siblings in Reading, England, and left school at sixteen. So when I started at a prep school nestled in hedgerows and surrounded by narrow country lanes, I didn't have any of the social or cultural reference points to contextualise my new classmates' lives. I interpreted them plainly. I saw their world with the expanse and clarity of a funky nineties camera with a fish-eye lens, close up but with a panoramic, panoptic view. I saw it for what it was: completely ridiculous and fucking weird.

Back then, I was trying to make sense of the behaviour of my peers. Why did their music taste differ so much from not just mine, but from my mum's, my cousins' and the kids' at my local playscheme? Why such disdain for council houses? Why didn't they know any black people? As I got older, the interrogative word shifted from *why* to *where*. Whether the lecture hall or the workplace, *where* were all the black people? And why did the workplace feel like an extension of a private school? The jokes, the reference points, the social activities, were all old hat to me but alienating for others. It's been over twenty years since I started school and, as you'd expect, my questions have changed in form, although one question underlies them all – what does class mean today, in twenty-first-century Britain? And how does racism complicate our understanding of class?

Rewind back to 1998: I am seven years old, dressed in my most fashionable outfit and am absolutely adorable. I'm about to gather eleven years of extensive evidence witnessing and documenting the movements of the middle classes of England and become a keen observer of the natives and their unfathomable activities. I am an intrepid explorer in a strange land. The middle class deserve their own ethnography and, unwittingly, I collected all the data.

• • •

'Getting to grips with the anthropology of the privileged classes is bruising and time-consuming . . . you don't get them from reading books or taking exams,' Conservative MP for Thurrock, Jackie Doyle-Price, told social mobility expert Duncan Exley for his book, *The End of Aspiration? Social Mobility and Our Children's Fading Prospects*.[2] In my experience, the immersive approach –

like being plonked in France with little vocabulary but leaving fluent in a new language – more or less does the trick.

My first introduction to the middle classes was through friendship. Mitra lived in a semi-detached mock-Tudor house in a cul-de-sac. We'd been friends since we were five, before I got the scholarship, and remain so. The house had a small conservatory that backed onto a garden with an apple tree. I know now that there are levels of posh that are only visible at closer inspection. There is middle and upper-middle, new money and the cash-poor aristocracy who know what a lounge suit or the 'right tie' is. To me, it was all the same thing. Having a semi-detached house and a garden was the height of sophistication and a clear marker of wealth. There were people who had money and people who didn't. And no matter. You can watch *The Rugrats* Chanukah specials on VHS and sing the Atomic Kitten version of 'Eternal Flame' in a house with a drive or in a tower block just the same.

The upper-middle class would be less forgiving, in my experience. On the top field, one day, stretching for athletics, one girl asked the rest of us to *imagine* living in council housing, as if it were equivalent to detention at Guantanamo. I knew to stay silent and laugh in the right places. Mum had prepared me for that, telling me before my first day, 'Don't tell anyone where you live.' She didn't want me to be mocked. There was nothing actually wrong with our flat. The rooms were a good size and well decorated. The communal areas needed repairs and investment. But I didn't question the logic of Mum's instructions because somehow I knew at age eight or nine that council housing said something about who you were and it was not positive. So I learnt to break my life up into fragments. I'd only show the shiniest parts and bury the blemished pieces.

I wasn't surprised by the comments about council housing. What was surprising and incomprehensible to me, however, was what was considered *cool.*

My new school had an unusual microclimate that didn't follow the national pattern. One afternoon, Mum was driving me home from school, from the Berkshire countryside to our estate, in our beat-up Peugeot 206.

'Celia is going to see ABBA with her parents. Everyone thinks it's cool,' I said, recounting the day's events in the art room.

'There is nothing cool about ABBA, Kim. Nothing at all.'

I didn't believe her at the time. Now I know the truth. ABBA songs bang, but cool, they are not. Only in a parallel universe could this be claimed and go unchallenged. Even by the end of my time at prep school no one listened to Kanye West. I listened to Nas on my Minidisc player and would trade it for the Red Hot Chili Peppers because only one other guy had a Minidisc player and that's what he listened to.

During this cultural apocalypse where everyone's parents seemed to listen to progressive rock, no one had heard of Blackstreet, or actually any nineties R&B except Usher and Destiny's Child. Maybe TLC at a stretch. Some garage cut through thanks to So Solid Crew's '21 seconds'. But no one seemed to know where the party was at, got weak in the knees or gave it up for the Westside. Cash ruled everything around them but no one had the C.R.E.A.M. Working knowledge of Dancehall was unthinkable, although Sean Paul had become popular.

Straight bops no one had heard of

- Tevin Campbell, 'Can We Talk'
- I-Wayne, 'Can't Satisfy Her'
- Mr Vegas, 'Heads High'
- Blackstreet (entire discography, someone asked if I meant Backstreet Boys)
- Next, 'Too Close'
- Cameo, 'Candy'
- Beenie Man, 'Dude'
- Bone Thugs-N-Harmony, 'Crossroads' (not the Blazin' Squad version)

There were things to learn from my years in the bastions of middle-class culture. I got a working knowledge of landfill indie music over the years. I got to go to Italy and attempt a sketch of Michelangelo's *David* and climbed a mountain in the Alps, which is pretty cool. And at least everyone watched *EastEnders*.

The 'comedy' show *Blackadder* baffled me. *Blackadder* is a BBC One pseudohistorical British 'sitcom' that ran for four series between 1983 and 1989, returning for one-off specials. It was written by the kings of middle-class culture: Rowan Atkinson, Richard Curtis and, later, Ben Elton. And until 2001, I had never heard of it. Yet teachers and pupils mentioned it repeatedly. At least that's how I remember it. Memories of how you stick out tend to be stickier.

At some point during 2001–2003, I would stumble across the show with my mum. We had recently got Sky Digital as a divorced parent version of pocket money from my dad. Flicking through the Woolworths' pick 'n' mix of channels, there it was – *Blackadder II*.

'People at school watch this show. The teachers love it,' I told Mum.

'Let's watch a bit. I bet it's rubbish.'

We lasted three minutes. It was a long three minutes with a lot of period costumes.

You don't have to be of a particular social class to enjoy *Blackadder*. But the cultural reference points it relies on, a base knowledge of historical events, particularly from the Regency and the Elizabethan period in its earlier seasons, can make it hard to follow if you don't have the required mental shortcuts. For this to be popular with ten- to thirteen-year-old children is weird.

It wasn't just music and telly where my reference points were a bit off. There were lots of things that didn't make sense to me. Particularly the art of doing things *just because*. People's parents would do a full shop at a Waitrose *just because*. People would go on Caribbean holidays, not because they had family there but just because they fancied it. They'd return, hair in braids with hair ties* at the ends to stop their straight strands from unravelling. At sports day, parents would rock up with HAMPERS. Fizz popped and guffaws ruffled the air with abandon. Gazebos were erected and mini barbecues were lit. Why wouldn't they just sit on a picnic mat with a homemade sandwich like normal people?

I also couldn't fathom the obsession with dogs. They *loved* their dogs. Why do they all know every breed of dog? 'Oh my god is that a Cockapoo cross?!' I'm sorry, WHAT? Why would you know that? Some kids even defended hunting foxes *for fun*, parroting their parents' views overheard at the dinner table. It was in the process of being partially banned by the government at the time.

Being posh means you can do the same things regular people do without being scolded, publicly shamed or having government departments start inquiries about it. You can do totally batshit stuff and everyone looks the other way.

Things posh people are allowed to do without judgement

- Have tattoos
- Have lots of dogs
- Have lots of kids
- Live in council flats in large urban centres (normally paid for with parental deposit)
- Wear tracksuits and gold hoops
- Wear costume jewellery
- Have a deep, raucous laugh
- Have names that lots of people can't pronounce or spell
- Look scruffy and unkempt in public (e.g. holes in clothes and shoes)
- Be racist

* See glossary page 20.

- Shop in charity shops/wear second-hand clothes
- Murder foxes for sport
- Do drugs
- Be an alcoholic
- Be unemployed
- Vote for Brexit*
- Be violent**
- Be loud
- Be emotionally constipated
- Be average

Mum made it clear that there were things that I could absolutely not get away with. When I got a school report that was mostly complimentary but said I had been talking a bit too much in class, she set me straight. These kids were going to grow up and their parents were going to help them in ways that she couldn't. They would get them jobs, invest in their fledgling businesses or make important introductions. They could afford distraction. In other words, I was broke and black and governed by a different set of rules. It was the well-worn chorus of the 'you have to work twice as hard' talk, the soundtrack to black childhood across the western hemisphere. And for a moment I hated her, because I knew it was true.

When I was at school, I didn't take much notice of being black if I could help it, unless forced to by a specific incident. I knew something in society was a bit off after the mid-week roast chicken and people having horse stables at their home. But I desperately

---

* They'll just say they're a libertarian.

** For example, the student studying medicine at Oxford who stabbed her boyfriend in the leg and threw objects at him, an offence that would normally carry a custodial sentence. The judge, Ian Pringle QC, faced criticism when he suggested she could potentially be spared a prison sentence because of her academic record, referring to her as 'an extraordinarily able young lady', https://www.independent.co.uk/news/uk/crime/lavinia-woodward-oxford-student-prison-jail-extraordinary-talent-10-months-suspended-sentence-stab-boyfriend-a7966486.html

wanted to believe that with hard work you could transcend racism because everyone would see how awesome you were. But those specific incidents would occur. They were infrequent but caused damage, like hailstorms, when they came.

Take Cassie – a very horsey girl – who called someone a 'black bastard' when I'd come round to play at about age ten. I do not remember the context, only the apology when she remembered who I was. This is the obvious kind of racism. The other kind is trickier to decipher at first.

The most difficult *this just doesn't feel right* stuff to make sense of were the insults that touched on race *and* class. Lance getting detention for saying my mum looked like a monkey is a case in point. To their credit, the school took it very seriously and even asked him if that was the way his parents spoke at home. This is not the case at every school and research has found that how racist bullying is dealt with is largely at the discretion of individual teachers.[3] Lance got detention and I knew why – racism is bad and crimes get punishments. It made sense. Racism deserved retribution. He also mentioned her gold tooth, which I now know to be associated with the working class. We weren't just black, we were *chavs*, which goes far beyond financial status but also encompasses 'a person's adherence to the establishment's rules of taste'.[4] My peers lived in the right neighbourhoods and their parents read the right newspapers. We didn't and that was worthy of ridicule to some of them.

Other things I picked up intuitively. We had a teacher known for terrible moral lessons. She told us a story about how as a child she felt better than the other girls in her neighbourhood, as she strode around in her grammar school uniform. This wasn't told as a cautionary tale about snobbery. When one day she asked us all what paper our parents read, I implicitly knew that 'no paper' was not the right answer. I had only heard of the *Sun* and we didn't buy the paper anyhow. She also asked us who our parents voted for, saying mine 'probably voted Labour'. (WRONG. My family didn't vote at all, although at the time were fans of Right to Buy.) I just said I didn't know.

I am glad the majority of my teachers were not like that. For instance, the maths teacher who didn't react when we were learning about negative numbers, and I, aged eight, gave the embarrassingly revealing example of an overdraft. She just said 'Yes it is' and moved on. I now know I should have gone with *thermometer*.

I learnt a crucial lesson about class – it's about a lot more than just money.

• • •

As a child I had a hunch that posh people liked very specific places, products and people. They believed that anything that fell outside of that was wrong and the way they chose to live was the correct approach. And they tended to like black people more if they behaved, dressed and spoke the same way they did. In 2013, a group of academics led by Professor Mike Savage launched the findings of a three-year project that would give some credence to my experiences. The Great British Class Survey had been commissioned by the BBC in 2011, and it had taken the academics two years to make sense of the 161,000 responses from the public. Influenced by the work of eminent French sociologist Pierre Bourdieu, they asked the British public a range of questions about their income and wealth (economic capital) but also their interests, tastes and activities and their social networks (cultural and social capital). From the analysis they assembled seven new classes that they felt were more reflective of the reality of class as it's lived in Britain today.[5]

Our cultural preferences – what we like to cook, wear, watch and listen to – are personal choices. But they are influenced by what our friends and colleagues think, and what the people we look up to enjoy, produce and reproduce. The tastes, behaviours and interests seen as legitimate, respectable and socially approved are associated with particular social classes.

From the survey, and accompanying in-depth interviews, the researchers found that having 'highbrow' tastes were not only associated with more privileged people but that it gave them the confidence to claim that their personal preferences constituted 'good' taste.[6] This isn't limited to opera and ballet but also includes activities like going to the theatre, museums, art galleries, restaurants and live music venues. A headteacher they interviewed beamed that he 'inflicted' his love of classical music on his students by playing it every morning as they filed in for assembly, even inferring that it could 'redeem' them.

'Most of what is judged to be beautiful, important, moving or intriguing will have been decided under circumstances that sought to censor and deride the experiences of low earners, for the purposes of upholding the logic and imperatives of social mobility,' Nathalie Olah writes in her book, *Steal as Much as You Can*. The people who decide what is 'tasteful', 'good quality' and 'respectable' are increasingly confined to the middle and upper-middle class.[7] For example, a 2018 study by Create London and the Universities of Sheffield and Edinburgh found the output of the creative industries had become more monocultural – making the same thing again and again since the 1970s – and mostly about the upper- and middle-class experience (think of infinite supply of period dramas about the aristocracy). Only 18.2 per cent of people working in music and performing and visual arts grew up in a working-class household. TV, radio, film and publishing all hover at 12–13 per cent.[8] More recent analysis published in November 2022, found a similar pattern to the Create London study. The proportion of actors, musicians and writers from a working-class background has shrunk by half since the 1970s.[9]

That's something that Sam Friedman, Professor of Sociology at the London School of Economics, uncovered in his own research with his colleague Daniel Laurison. They both worked on the British Class Survey with Professor Mike Savage and then went on to write their own book, *The Class Ceiling: Why it Pays to be Privileged*. 'When you talk to people about their career narratives in lots of occupations, particularly cultural and creative, where the labour market's particularly precarious and uncertain, having that insulation of parental wealth is just absolutely pivotal,' he told me. Friedman and Laurison went into three prestigious workplaces – a multinational accountancy firm, an architecture practice and Channel 4 – and observed how class affected everything from which departments people worked in to what was considered 'cool' and who was seen as a future leader.[10] 'At Channel 4, so many people I spoke to had sort of come off the creative tightrope, which would get you to the commissioning room eventually' (where they decide which TV shows to produce). Instead he found they had gone into 'safer' parts of the business. 'They've gone into admin, they've gone into sales, they've gone into technical areas, because it was more financially secure,' he said. This affects not only the careers and earning potential of staff without parents who can support them financially. It also affects the kind of shows that get made and limits the range of content on our screens.

There is, however, a generational chasm between what is considered cool, influential and culturally relevant. Regardless, it is still middle- and upper-middle-class gatekeepers who get to decide. But while the headteacher favours classical music, Professor Savage found that young, better-off and well-educated people had more eclectic taste in music, TV and activities, although they were still very selective about it. They would watch *Love Island*, but defend the choice by justifying why – calling it a guilty pleasure or qualifying it by writing an essay in the *Guardian* likening the show to an anthropological study. Showing your range is what counts. This isn't a problem in and of itself – people like what they like! It becomes an issue when personal preferences and arbitrary behaviour become de facto measures of intelligence, talent and potential. 'The classic is speaking in RP (received pronunciation or "Queen's English"),' Friedman told me. 'So being read as sort of unflappable and softly spoken. And the point with this stuff is that it's really linked to class background. You talk to people from working-class backgrounds, and they say, my working-class accent is routinely read as a sign [that] I am too passionate. I'm too aggressive.'

In 2018, Faiza Shaheen, then the Director of the think-tank CLASS and now Visiting Professor in Practice at LSE, was experiencing an extreme version of what Professor Friedman described. During an appearance on Sky News, she was mocked by the journalist Adam Boulton on Twitter for her diction and pronunciation of words. She grew up in East London in a working-class family. It wasn't the first or last time she'd had a strong response to how she speaks.

'When I started going on TV, I just would get flooded with all of these tweets to say you don't speak properly, you don't do your Ts. It was quite substantial,' she said. 'They would say things like, "You need to learn how to speak properly. My mum used to call people like you slags." It was so mad.' She once had a very revealing back-and-forth with a random man online: he asked her why she doesn't pronounce her Ts. 'This is how I sound like because we don't learn to say our Ts at East London state schools,' she told him. 'And he was like, "Well, I wouldn't mind so much if you weren't talking about politics. I expect that on *Match of the Day*."' After TV appearances, she would receive letters and phone calls to the office telling her to 'speak properly'.[11] The letters and phone calls would also often be littered with racist abuse (Faiza has Fijian and Pakistani heritage). In response to a tweet about Faiza 'dropping her Ts' on Sky News, Boulton suggested that 'dropping [them] shows you are embarrassed about being posh.'[12] 'Statistically, maybe it was probably more likely that I was putting it on, than legitimately from that background,' she said. He later apologised.

When Shaheen took up a post at New York University (NYU) and moved to the US, she noticed a shift. 'I've really noticed here because people don't know my accent, they just think I've got a British accent. So I don't get class prejudice. I've noticed it in the workplace.'

I've been speaking in RP since age six (according to Mum I picked it up from my best friend Mitra only to take it up a notch at prep school and scale it back at uni). I have been treated more favourably because of it. It's not just the accent, though. It's knowing what to say, when, and how. With the deployment of the right term at the right time, you can transform from scary-black-person to not-at-all-threatening by simply saying 'prep time' or 'junior common room'. And of course, never saying anything directly and speaking mostly in euphemism, especially when talking about things and people you don't like. The aim is to obfuscate.

Glossary of posh terms: from boarding school to the boardroom

Aga Posh stove and oven that's hard to turn off so it's just on all the time

Au pair A young person from mainland Europe no older than twenty-four who looks after posh people's children. Family not rich enough for a nanny

Centre Parcs Middle-class Butlin's

Cornwall, the Cotswolds and the Caribbean Locations of second homes

Common Entrance (13+) An exam in Year 8 that only prep school kids take to get into another private school. Similar to 11+ for grammar school but even more exclusionary and outdated

Doing pretty well/being comfortable/financial cushion Having no money worries and having never seen or heard of a prepaid electricity meter or a bailiff but not wanting to show off about it. Actually top 1 per cent of earners in England and Wales. See also 'Well off' below

Hair ties Hair bands

Henley regatta Boat racing for poshos. All the worst people from across the Anglophone world converge on Henley, Berkshire, to race boats or watch them go. Students from American Ivy Leagues who row fly in for the occasion. Despite the heat men still wear formal jackets. Excuse to get pissed. Astoundingly average Mayfair nightclub Mahiki has a bar in the enclosure

New money People who made money by working for it rather than inheriting it. Don't conform to the tastes preferred by older money. Outdated term

Octavia and Rupert Names of children

'Oh my God, you've NEVER BEEN SKIING?!' You are so rich you cannot fathom that most people in Britain have never been skiing because it's very expensive

Part-loan a horse You can't afford to own a horse full time so you borrow one once a week from a richer person

Prep Homework

Ski season Posh people 'work' (get pissed) in a chalet on their gap year in Val d'Isère/Val Thorens, France, and then all reconvene at the University of Exeter/St Andrews/Warwick the next year

Tiffany and Thomas Sabo bracelets Tacky but popular late nineties and early noughties status symbols for young women. Was height of sophistication

Teaching English as a foreign language (TEFL) Young person with no discernible talent for teaching benefits from British imperialism, American cultural hegemony and the consequent domination of the English language to go abroad and 'teach' English. Normally use cash to fund their travels. Qualify by taking an online course

Urban Codeword for things black people create or like, such as clothing and music and club nights that you're both slightly afraid of but also think are cool. Preference is to engage with 'urban' culture but with as few actual black people present as possible (one to two maximum for edginess)

Weekly boarder Someone who lives at school on weekdays but goes home at the weekend

Well off Very fucking rich. Inherited wealth

Like any dialect, the more you become immersed in the local culture, the better your proficiency. You pick it up as you go until you're fluent. And once you sound the part and look the part, you're sorted. By 2004, I'd leveraged my first scholarship into a second. I knew what to namecheck in the interview: my attempt to sketch Michelangelo's *David* and penchant for nineteenth-century literature. My secondary school was also private but the people were much more worldly. They had heard of Kanye West and watched *Run's House* on MTV. Some of my friends even lived in council flats and were also on financial aid! We'd moved into a two-up terrace whose design didn't scream social housing, so I started inviting people over to stay. I could finally breathe and used that extra energy to have disdain for other working-class people who weren't 'doing it right'.

This disdain wasn't because I was uniquely self-important. These years were the height of multiple moral panics, notably chavs and hoodies. Everyone was at it: MPs across the political spectrum, TV producers, journalists and commentators.[13] *The Jeremy Kyle Show* launched in 2005 and by 2007 had been described by Manchester district judge, Alan Berg, as 'a human form of bear baiting'.[14] In an article for *New Statesman*, journalist Anoosh Chakelian said the show 'curates a morbidly chaotic picture of a British underclass – for those watching at home to scoff and sneer at – with the veneer of helping them'.[15] It was cancelled in 2019 following the suspected death by suicide of a guest,[16] although at the time of writing this essay, Kyle has a new show on TalkTV.[17] 2005 also saw the launch of the comically classist reality show, *Ladette to Lady*, where self-proclaimed ladettes (women who are 'crude' and drink boisterously) were sent to a finishing school.[18]

In a speech in the run-up to the 2001 general election, Tony Blair made a speech on education and meritocracy. 'As a nation, we are wasting too much of the talent of too many of the people,' he said. 'The mission of any second term must be this: to break down the barriers that hold people back, to create real upward mobility, a society that is open and genuinely based on merit and the equal worth of all.'[19] Seeking re-election in 2005, he announced a crackdown on 'disrespect and yobbish behaviour. People are tired of street-corner and shopping-centre thugs.'[20] Between the options of chav, hooded thug or upward mobility, only one was appealing.

So I laughed at *Jeremy Kyle* guests, laughed when someone branded them as *plebs* and called things 'chavvy' as if five years previously I hadn't been one. I would wear my working-class identity from time to time, but only to foreground my ascension beyond it.

One of my favourite teachers, my English teacher, declared in one of our classes that we were all middle class (to make a valid point about privilege as far as I recall). I defiantly made it clear that I was not silver-spooned like so many of my peers. Though the pride wasn't in where I'd started in life but that I had left it behind, with what I believed back then to be perseverance and grit. It was easier to believe in meritocracy, that my ability plus effort brought my successes. It discounted the role chance played in me changing school in my early life or the impact the small class sizes and school trips had on my development.

This isn't to say that I didn't face more financial and social barriers than most of my peers throughout my early life. In some sense, those experiences will forever live within me. But slowly and unconsciously, my cultural reference points, clothes and speech pattern had changed until I was largely indistinguishable from the rest of my friendship group by the time I was fourteen. I've been benefitting from that ever since and to deny it would be dishonest.

Professor Friedman told me this phenomenon is pretty common. 'People, whether consciously or not, want to tell a kind of meritocratic story about themselves in order to be seen as legitimate,' he said. 'Claiming humble origins is a way of saying that your destination is more meritocratic.' The 'self-made' billionaire origin story is a classic of this myth-making genre. Jeff Bezos founds a plucky start-up called Amazon.com in a suburban garage and becomes a tech-titan, so the story goes.[21] It leaves out the $245,000 his mum and stepdad invested to get it off the ground.[22] But regular people are at it too. In interviews with a range of people on class, Friedman and his colleagues found that people who had middle-class upbringings would commonly downplay their advantages by drawing on their grandparents' 'striving' or other family stories of the past, often defensively. For example, a senior partner at an architecture practice whose dad was also an architect, focused more on the fact that his grandmother had worked in a mill than on his father's job and how that may have contributed to his own success.[23] 'Regardless of the intentionality of the person, it's relevant because it's acting to sort of blind those individuals from reflecting,' Friedman added.

This might feel counterintuitive. On social media and in progressive social circles, it can feel like people are falling over themselves to declare their race and class privilege. It is commonly found in the introduction to millennial-orientated books, on popular podcasts and as a pinned comment 'disclaimer' under TikToks. I don't think this is bad. It's good, actually. But acknowledging something isn't the same as interrogating it. While downplaying racial advantage is the purview of right-wing reactionaries with tiresome newspaper columns and radio guest spots, the incentive to downplay class advantage is two-fold: to feel we earned our good fortune and to come across as relatable.

In a hate-click article for *Elle* magazine titled, 'I'm A Millionaire But I Pretend That I'm Broke', the anonymous author tells readers that she pretends to be a struggling creative living in East London, when she is in fact 'filthy rich'. She claims to have changed her accent and says 'Fuck Boris' in chorus with friends, when her dad actually went to school with him and she thinks he's quite nice. Her defence is that the extremely posh circles she was born into – aristocratic levels of wealth – are very boring. 'Just because someone is on my level financially, doesn't make them interesting,' she writes.[24] The article is so over the top it reads like fabricated copy. But real or fake, it touches on the very real desire to be relatable and romanticise struggle.

While it may be fashionable for middle-class people to wear Adidas tracksuits or buy an ex-local-authority flat now, I spent my teens running away from all working-class signifiers. I wasn't ashamed of being black but I was ashamed of being poor. This is as deeply embarrassing as it is true. I did things 'properly' and if other black people simply did the same they would do well too. I had swallowed whole the respectability narrative, that black people just needed to take their hoodies off and 'be articulate' and then all our ills would evaporate. Being embarrassed of your teenage self is normal and I stand by some of my decisions, like dropping Chemistry AS, my friendship group and a growing appreciation for the indie music that'd begun to top the charts.

After my brief flirtation with the Red Hot Chili Peppers Minidisc in 2003, I made a natural progression from American rock to landfill indie. The airways vibrated with the words of mostly white boys whining mostly about women: gals looking good on the dancefloor, guys with the same jeans on for four days, and giving zero fucks about Oxford commas. It's what a lot of middle-class people at Berkshire private schools liked at the time. And no harm done.

Big tunes were made. It's also prepared me well for the disco section of white, middle-class weddings.

In 2019, on a bad date with a guy I'd met at a sex club – a setting I can testify is not one to pick up dates – he asked me if I listened to Oasis. He was black, and having told him I went to school with predominantly white people, he presumed that was the kind of thing I might have listened to.

There is nothing inherently 'white' about liking Oasis. Or even a band with Waspy-infused lyrics like Vampire Weekend. There is a term for that and it's called cultural essentialism. People are free to like any genre of music. Although as a shorthand and for comedic effect I'd definitely describe bands like Sports Team and Vampire Weekend as 'the whitest bands on earth'. Being black and liking any of these bands also doesn't make you special.

There are reasons why sex club guy asked me if I like Oasis and why indie night at uni was basically all white people. My friend (who is white) claimed that Factory was the easiest place to pull but this was not the case for me. I could never pull at indie night at Factory but had no trouble at Joshua Brooks on a Wednesday, where hip-hop was played. I didn't need a kiss when I could just scream Courteeners' lyrics anyway, but I noted the pattern privately.

In 2020, journalist and author Raven Smith shared an extract from his book, *Trivial Pursuits*, in a piece in the *Observer* about his relationship with his father and race. He had grown up mostly with his white mother and stepfather in a very comfortable setting. He described himself as 'pigmentally Jamaican' and went on to say: 'As I gaze around me at the white middle-class paraphernalia, my amassed signifiers of success, I know I am culturally white. That's not to say there are no successful black people on the same page as me, but I haven't lived out the reductive story of blocked opportunity so often associated with inner-city black men.'[25]

My corner of Twitter winced. Sharing your personal story publicly online is hard enough as it is. And Twitter isn't known for good-faith conversations or analysis. I for one have worked through my racial identity online through writing and received 'feedback' from strangers on social media that I did not appreciate (some of it, in hindsight, was accurate, but I wasn't ready for those conversations). So at least from a corner of Twitter – a weird mash up of black journalists, pop-culture commentators and academics – people were quietly critical.

But not having lived out that a journey of socioeconomic struggle, repeated overt racism and liking fancy things doesn't make you culturally white. It makes you middle class (or in this case upper class by the sounds of it – he mentioned a family boat) and your tastes and interests match that. You're just a product of your environment.

In an interview on the *Growing up with gal-dem* podcast, broadcaster Clara Amfo talked about the reductive way the experiences of black British people are understood. 'A lot of people project expectations of the "black experience" in so many different ways,' she said. 'I think there are people who still don't understand that there are black people who go to private school, and not on scholarships but because their parents are loaded. But I think we've been fed this narrative that all black people are working class and have grown up in social housing. And nothing else. There's a very limited and monolithic conversation around how black people are brought up.'

In her stand-up show on class, comedian Athena Kugblenu called this phenomenon the 'black person origin story'. As a black woman (half Indo-Guyanese and half Ghanaian) in comedy, she said she gets asked to edit scripts about life on council estates and to give advice to up-and-coming working-class writers. The problem is she grew up in a three-bed semi-detached in East Finchley, North London. Her parents arrived in the UK as young professionals from Guyana and Ghana respectively but experienced significant downward mobility – they couldn't get jobs that matched their qualifications. Her mum was a dinner lady and her dad struggled to find anything and sometimes took work in Ghana instead. Her life isn't easily contained within a simple story and doesn't slot neatly into the limited narratives on offer.[26]

'When you get a famous black person they're never just like a famous black person,' she said on the BBC Radio 4 edition of her set. 'They're always a famous black person who came from a single-parent household and had to struggle. It's true that we should talk about our backgrounds honestly but making struggle synonymous with black people is a falsehood.'[27]

Not all black people are on low incomes. I knew this to be true because I'd met middle-class black people at school. There are, however, proportionally more black people on low incomes in Britain than white people. This often encourages a conflation of race and class, because one narrative takes precedence and crowds out the others. It's hard to tell the story of a community that is marginalised, to speak of a 'we' and an 'us', without flattening the differences that constitute the 'I' of our individual lives.

• • •

My secondary school took a group of selected students to tour Oriel College, Oxford. I was one of them, and Mum was excited by the prospect. On the tour, everything that was sold to us as enticing looked exclusionary to me. Imposing spires and Hogwarts-like dining halls with specific codes of dress. A statue of the prince of precious gem extraction and the ravenous exploitation of black people, Cecil Rhodes, stood imposingly over the college's main entrance. I knew I didn't want this life. Unforgivably, when I asked a student whether people went out clubbing a lot in Oxford (an informal university ranking I was making in my head) she responded with the deal breaker: 'Not really. We mostly go to pubs.' There was no way I was moving to a city without a strong club culture. I love pubs but I'd spent my teens dreaming about clubbing. There was a video for an under-eighteens club night that I watched over and over again until my dreams were infused with the garage beats of 'Imagine' by Shola Ama (Asylum remix). The actual club night was crap of course, held in our local leisure centre. But I knew the real ones would be better – I just had to wait. At seventeen, I snuck into a club with a friend by arriving so early the bouncer's shift hadn't started. I got a highly dubious fake student card for an invented university and used it to slink into clubs in Spain. I stood on a podium and let myself dissolve into the blue lights and frenetic tempo of 'Show Me Love' by Robin S and thought, yes, this is what it means to be alive.

Earlier that year, I'd unexpectedly caught non-pulmonary tuberculosis. It's a medical mystery and no one knows how I got it, only that it was as unlikely as it was unlucky. I prayed to survive and promised myself I'd live my life in a new way. I'm not sure I would have had the confidence to make the decisions that made me happy instead of what was expected of me otherwise. And credit to my mum, she supported all of my choices. The brush with mortality made me ravenous for living. I wanted to be where music played in the streets. I took a gap year and went backpacking in South America, where the music played loudly. It was 2010, the same year that *gap yah** YouTube video became a meme that would blight the freshers of History and PPE students across the UK. Or as I wrote in my travel diary at the time:

* The name given to the year or often a longer period of time that posh kids spend travelling the world using Daddy's money after leaving their expensive private school. Immortalised by the quality 'Unexpected Items' YouTube video mocking the higher classes of society, https://www.urbandictionary.com/define.php?term=Gap%20Yah

Gap yahs

> Thanks to our good friend YouTube a satirical sketch on the typical gap year preppy snob has been linked to us by Noah's sister via Facebook. The girls from the north [of England] said they were in their hostel discussing what jobs they'd worked before travelling. Everyone listed various bar work and waitressing gigs when it got to a posh British lad who complained: 'Well Daddy sent me to Dubai to map oil rigs, and he didn't help me at all!' He was 100 per cent serious. This is the stereotype we have to battle with.

Unfortunately, the video went viral. When I got to uni and admitted I'd gone on a gap year, my flatmates rinsed me for the entirety of our first semester.

For a lot of ethnic minorities, university is a culture shock, which is sometimes traumatic. As Yomi Adegoke notes in the book, *Slay in Your Lane*, for many black students, university is their first experience of 'living in a predominantly white area or environment [where] Black music was relegated to a Thursday night and primarily consisted of Sean Paul's discography'.[28] Racist stereotyping and assumptions may mar the experience but, at its worst, students of colour face racist bullying and discrimination, which has finally started coming to light in recent years.[29]

With each rung up the metaphorical ladder of my life the disparities between black and white people got larger and larger. The only respite from this was at the University of Manchester. This is not because Manchester is an anti-racist socialist utopia. Like all Russell Group universities (research intensive institutions with elite status), if you're black you're less likely to apply, get in, or get a first or 2:1 even if you start with the same grades as your white peers.[30] It's just that, compared to school, Manchester University was like a historically black US college. The bar was pretty low. There were only six people of colour in my year at secondary school and I was one of two black British people. I studied History, a course where only 11 per cent of undergraduate students were from a Black or Minority Ethnic (BME) backgrounds in 2018.[31] But Manchester was still an improvement. You could meet people who grew up in London and Birmingham, which was very exciting. The clubs were great and lots of people knew the lyrics to hip-hop, R&B and Dancehall hits.

I also learnt some stuff while I was there that would help me finally answer a persistent hum of questions. I did undergraduate modules on identity and migration and imperialism and borrowed the language, the theory and evidence of the past until they became an instrumental track that I layered the lyrics of my life on top of. But it was my master's at the London School of Economics that turned the volume up from a hum to a scream. The lack of black British people studying there shocked me, which made me ask myself, why?

My gran – who emigrated to Britain from Jamaica and was taught that the streets in Britain were paved with gold – got spat at in the street in 1960s Reading. People would ask if she had a tail. When my mum was at school a teacher asked a black student to get on the table and act like a monkey 'as a joke'. This isn't forgotten history consigned to a distant time – this was the 1960s and 1980s. Racism and division may feel a new tragedy, a momentary lapse in judgement by a normally well-adjusted country, a blip that started in 2016 with the Brexit referendum campaign but isn't representative of who we really are. But racism has always been a defining feature of the country, and our EU neighbours too.[32]

My mum's side of the family had a fairly typical journey to England. My gran moved in 1960 as part of the Windrush generation. We're a rural, farming family. Research shows that black people who moved from the Caribbean were more likely to have done blue-collar or farming work back home than people who moved from African countries during the 1960s to 1990s.[33] Many black African people were from middle-class families, came to the UK to study and then stayed.[34] Yet both generations of both groups failed to get jobs that matched their skills, even for the generation raised in Britain.[35] For black Caribbean and African men in particular, having parents in 'high-status' jobs and having a degree still leaves them disadvantaged compared to their white peers of a similar background.[36] These are people with very different starting points, different stories. They are united by the colour of their skin. We know that discrimination is happening. The extensive CV studies – where names that sound 'ethnic' get fewer responses from employers than white ones – make that clear. Europe is no better either, with Germany, the Netherlands, Norway and Spain all found to discriminate against particular minority groups in their respective countries in similar ways.[37]

The inequality that we see isn't randomly patterned. But patterns without context look like inevitabilities. They appear innate. They are read as personal failures and they end up shaping not only public attitudes but the way we see ourselves. Put another way, the system is rigged but individuals get blamed.

Some of the obstacles in the way of young professionals from working-class backgrounds are hard to quantify. It's access to social networks that can help you score an internship. It's the 'knowing' behaviours needed to get ahead or what academic Sheamus Khan calls *ease*: the skills required to get ahead in corporate and professional environments that can't really be taught.[38] It's the tastes and behaviours I picked up in school that have served me well at work.

In most of my graduate jobs so far, where the dominant culture has been middle class, white and liberal, I've found it easy to make friends and connect with others. I genuinely enjoy organising payday socials and after-work drinks. This isn't to say I didn't take issue with how these organisations were run or the work they did. One of my former employers had a reckoning on racism, sexism and classism that resulted in the CEO being sacked and a very public culture review. But my career progression wasn't personally impacted by the workplace culture because it mimicked the environments I'd grown up in. I love BBC political comedy *The Thick of It* and was a co-founder of the cheese and port club. I fit right in.

This isn't true for a lot of black people, who are more likely to be from a low-income family or have different cultural reference points depending on where they grew up. I'll never forget a friend who told me that a black woman at his employer had quit before she was pushed. She saw the synopsis of what lay ahead in loaded comments like 'You're not a team player' and other vague claims in which no evidence was presented. In 2022, broadcaster Richie Brave tweeted that his friend, the only black person at a company, was let go during their probationary period for 'not being the right fit', despite performing well at the tasks they were given. The thread was littered with black people, especially black women, saying they had experienced something similar. A black man even added to the thread: 'Not the right fit' always equals something along the lines of 'You never attend work drinks' or 'You never come to the pub at lunch.'[39]

In a survey of over 2000 women of colour, black women of African heritage were most likely to change the clothes they wear, the language they use, the topics they talk about, their hairstyle or accent to fit in and get ahead at work than any other group. Black women of Caribbean heritage were the least likely to feel comfortable in their workplace culture.[40] In-depth interviews with a spectrum of women, from entry level to senior leadership, lay bare a pattern of women of colour inexplicably sidelined in favour of white male and female colleagues with less experience and qualifications. They felt dominant ideas of 'leadership fit' held them back. Experiences like senior leaders being mistaken for the secretary or hospitality staff at high-level meetings reinforced these feelings.

'I am a black woman, I don't straighten my hair, I speak with a London accent,' one of the case studies, Janine, said. 'It has never been a question of my competence – but fundamentally to do with how I look and the perceptions that people have of me. We think that people get their jobs because of merit – people believe that even though it is so obviously not true.'[41]

We need to disentangle the superfluous things that get misread as merit – being the last one standing at payday drinks, sharing the same sense of humour, enjoying holidays on the Amalfi Coast – and actually being good at your job.

• • •

I stopped feeling working class when in the autumn of 2011 I was living in a nine-bed dive in Fallowfield, Manchester, in the worst house, at the best university in the best city in the world, after the best house party there'd ever been. I'd had sex with the hottest guy I'd ever met whose Facebook page I showed to anyone who cared, or did not care, to see. Seven of us tangled together on the spare mattress. Its repurposing, from mattress, to weed-smoking chill-out zone, to come-down recovery centre, further proved that there was something supernatural about this city. We ate ice lollies to chill our fevers. I laughed at the comedy playing on the boxy TV I'd bought for £1 on eBay. The show was *Blackadder Goes Forth*. I couldn't deny it any more. It was over. I wasn't acting. I hadn't been for a long time.

I wouldn't dare to claim a working-class identity now – it does not feel legitimate. I have some semblance of economic security and access to impenetrable institutions my grandmother Daphne would never have had. As a master's student I moved into a listed building, a tower block in East London, Balfron Tower. It is famous for its Marxist architect, Ernő Goldfinger, and an iconic photo of grime artist Dizzee Rascal stood in front of it. Now though, my moving in meant pushing out the families like mine. The building was providing a stopgap for young professionals like me, and artists, so that the flats could be redeveloped and sold privately (a sale and refurb that's now complete). Popular Harca, the housing association responsible for the regeneration of the Brownfield estate, claims that 95 per cent of former residents were rehoused within Tower Hamlets, with 81 per cent in Harca-owned properties.[42] Critic and author Owen Hatherley, who writes primarily about architecture, called the process at Balfron Tower, 'a pure description of how [gentrification] works in practice'.[43]

If you're potentially complicit in the social cleansing of a tower block, you're probably not working class any more. To call myself working class feels outrageous. I could maybe say 'working-class background' – past tense – if I had to say something. I don't wish to erase the past as if having been working class is a shameful thing. But materially, I cannot and should not be claiming kinship with the day-to-day realities of Deliveroo drivers fighting for employment rights or university cleaners who are unionising and organising.

This does not stop, say, Lord Alan Sugar from invoking the identity. In April 2019, in response to comments about his criticism of Jeremy Corbyn's policies, he tweeted: 'I am working class lad [sic] and have always been contrary to what your perception you may have of me.'[44] He expressed similar sentiments in 2017.[45]

A billionaire can be working class?

How sensible is it to allow and normalise the claim of a billionaire with a fifteen-year (and counting) TV series to be working class? What does he have in common with 90 per cent of the country, let alone the worst-off? We have to break apart our understanding of class and rebuild it so it actually reflects how we live now.

Most British people shy away from claiming a more privileged identity. The Great British Class Survey discovered not three classes – working, middle and upper – but seven that define modern Britain. After my graduation, I sat in the 'emergent service worker' category. This group is predominantly well-educated young people, who have yet to accumulate large amounts of economic capital. Ethnic minorities are well represented in this group. Professor Mike Savage and his team noted that many ethnic minorities had accumulated large amounts of social and cultural capital (like going to university) but had not been able to translate this into actual money or security.[46] We are also well represented in the precariat – the poorest people in the country. I took the test again and, as of writing, I'm still an emergent service worker. I rent my home, have some savings (I'm probably at the higher end of the salary band), hang out with a wide range of people and like cultural activities outside of the home.

I want to be as honest as I can be about my position. But in a survey commissioned by the Great British Class Survey team, 62 per cent of participants identified as working class in some form, with 41 per cent describing themselves as 'middle working class'. But in the UK nearly one in four people in middle-class jobs from middle-class backgrounds – approximately 3.5 million people – see themselves as working class.[47] The urge to associate with working-class identities even when it doesn't match your reality is pervasive.[48] In 2022 *New Statesman* found that more than one in five of people earning between £75,000 and £100,000 identified as working class. A salary of £75,000 would put you in the top 6 per cent of taxpayers in 2019–20.[49]

Dr Faiza Shaheen, Visiting Professor in Practice at LSE, thinks defining class identity can be difficult if someone's life has changed over time. 'I know a lot of work people from working-class backgrounds where after a while, [they] only have middle-class people around them. But if someone lives in the area they grew up in and has a similar social network, it's not unreasonable for them to still consider themselves working class even if, financially, they're not,' she said. 'When you claim to be working class still when you don't live that life any more, you know, if you're Alan Sugar and have the money and the power, then you're trying to legitimise yourself as a working-class voice but you're not. Especially when it's been years.'

I'm certain Lord Alan Sugar would qualify as the elite if he took this test (he may have already!). Perhaps he holds onto his identity from a reactive sense of displacement – all the subtle slights experienced on the way up, the papercuts of snobbery that mark any story of 'social mobility'. In the Great British Class survey, time and time again people who had made a class jump had a 'debilitating feeling that they would fall at any moment', exposed as a 'fraud'. If people treat you like an imposter you will feel like one. It's not a syndrome, we're not ill.

Additionally, feelings of exclusion shouldn't be ignored. We do need language that can speak to that feeling of alienation, like you're still an outsider even when your life has changed beyond recognition. But feelings alone shouldn't determine how policies are made, how political parties carry out analysis and make decisions, or how journalists write and frame stories. The emotional is important but it isn't empirical. We should measure what we can, knowing it's imperfect. Like Professor Friedman did, we should look at class origin – the jobs our parents did – which can affect how well people do in the job market. He found that if your parents were doing a routine manual job, say a cleaner, labourer, call centre worker or being long-term unemployed, that even when people get high-status jobs, you still go on to earn about 16 per cent less than your colleagues.

It isn't perfect. It's still reductive – all our searches for patterns are. It gives us a broad, albeit fuzzy, picture. People's class backgrounds are messy because life can change so much in just childhood alone. But if you grew up with your architect dad and you're also an architect, you're not working class – sorry!

Dr Faiza Shaheen described her current class background in frank terms. 'I can't say I'm working class any more. But at the same time, it was such an important part of my formative years. For me. It's my— it's the window that I look out to see the world.'

I used to think I was special and that my story was unique. There is nothing unique about my social mobility story at all. An improbable event outside of my control, mentorship and support from teachers and, most importantly of all, healthy relationships with family, a semi-functioning social security system and stable, long-term tenancies in social housing with genuinely affordable rents, is very much in line with research on life chances and aspiration.

Social mobility as it's currently sold is a con. It supposes that you have everything to gain and nothing to lose by changing yourself in order to succeed. It made me feel ashamed of where I was born and where I lived. It made me judge my family members' behaviour when there was nothing wrong with it. Sure, they're a bit loud and quite blunt but that's not a crime. Being loud and direct would be called 'spirited' and 'passionate' if another demographic were doing it. 'No one I spoke to wanted to attain social mobility,' says Duncan Exley in a summary of his book on the subject. 'They just wanted to pursue opportunities not normally attained by people of their background.'[50] The chance to live a life not determined by where you were born. To be treated with respect.

• • •

The world today looks different to how it did in 1998 when I was a hesitant seven-year-old about to enter a new paradigm of British life.

But some things never change. Judgement and entitlement are everywhere. The paradox of my work, which has taken me into Parliament and on to television, is that my schooling, all those early years in the countryside, has greatly enabled my career progression. It got me used to some of its defining features: wealth, entitlement, whiteness. But I still don't feel fully comfortable in those spaces and it has not meant I have been treated well. I have been barked at in Parliament and dismissed by senior civil servants. I have stumbled out of the Royal Society of Arts and onto the Strand, stiff upper lip quivering but held in place until I'm on the bus home where I can safely let the tears leak. I've changed, but the world around me hasn't moved forward at the same pace.

If people just want to pursue opportunities not normally attained by people of their background, then there is an attitudinal issue that becomes a systemic one. These attitudes can exist in anyone but proliferate in elite circles and the established middle class. It's the pretentious belief that you *should* lead, *should* be deferred to, and that everyone *should* want to be like you. This may have implicitly been reinforced every day of your life – on television, in school and at work.

In an episode of the 2019 reality show *When I Grow Up* on Channel 4, six primary school children from a variety of socio-economic backgrounds take over *Hello!* magazine for two weeks. One child, Charlie, who is middle class with a self-professed 'goal-setting' father, dominates every scenario he is put in. When Samuel, a black child who has lost confidence following bullying so extensive he had to move school, gets to be in the limelight, Charlie cannot help but try and overshadow him. By the end of the episode, Charlie has learnt that the best way to get things done well is 'all about teamwork and you have to use other people's ideas and not just yours. Your ideas aren't always correct.' It is the perfect microcosm. Life is not a reality show, with producers and child psychologists on hand to help us reflect. What it does tell us, though, is that 'empowering' working-class children to increase their aspirations is not going to change what our society looks like. The Charlies of the world need to learn to make space for other people and value them, their ideas and experiences too.

The assumption that middle-class behaviours and tastes are the norm to be measured against and assimilated into is also archaic and obnoxious. Being offered opportunities and enabled to take them, say, an art gallery doing an outreach programme, is a good thing. This is very different to the paternalistic 'inflicting' of your classical music taste on students.

• • •

The joke of meritocracy is that the more tests we create to sort people by their supposed ability, the more wealthy parents will buy their children the training needed to either pass them, or to circumvent these obstacles entirely if they fail. It's the extracurriculars that help kids seem 'well-rounded' and tutors hired if they are falling behind. Some of these tests come later and are based on personality and popularity; the nebulous ability to 'fit in'. This can be knowing which suit or trainers to wear (when to dress up and when to dress down), enjoying adventure holidays and trading tips over lunch, or having gone to the same university as your peers. They are not predictors of job performance but get read that way. We need to start getting more comfortable talking about advantage without qualifying it. Lots of us work hard, but it doesn't get us all to the same place.

We will never have actual equality of opportunity (and certainly not outcomes) within capitalism because some advantaged parents will continue to do whatever it takes to help their children. That's fine – people love their kids. I empathise particularly with black parents, who see headlines like 'Exclusion rates five times higher for black Caribbean pupils in parts of England' and 'Black youth unemployment rate of 40 per cent, data shows', see a government and opposition offering little in response, and take their children out of the state system.[51] But that's an individual response to a structural problem because very few people can afford to do that.

Most people only have power over their personal attitudes and how they treat people in their day-to-day lives. Perhaps, they can influence their friends and family too. It's the responsibility of the government and workplaces to do the rest, including mitigating the fallibility of individuals with policies.

If we eliminated all forms of discrimination and vastly limited the power of family wealth and connections – in other words, if the system weren't as rigged – British society would be much better for it. But we need more than that.

I know how much I've benefitted from unearned advantage – my mum teaching me to read and write at age three, private school and skills that we happen to value in the job market – and it humbles me. It stops me being a dickhead. I am still proud of my achievements. I just know they're not simply down to 'genius' or 'grit'. Knowing the system is rigged motivates me. The adage 'Have the confidence of a mediocre, middle-class white man', the clarion call against imposter syndrome, works because it acknowledges that the playing field is not level and your lot in life is not simply down to effort.

But by banging on about social mobility and meritocracy, we ignore the more important question. Making things fairer, like access to elite universities and professions, is admirable and important. But we need a society that is just as well as fair. When all the attention is on the 'talented' (whatever that means, and whoever gets to decide what that means), its implicit meaning is that inequality in and of itself is just. For every poor kid classed as 'gifted' who deserves a break, is another deemed 'not academic' or 'difficult' – perhaps facing permanent exclusion from school – who deserves support and opportunity, respect and dignity, a fulfilling life and financial security, too.

Professor Friedman told me we need to increase the value and dignity associated with working-class jobs. 'That means, pay, conditions and through softer ways, like the prestige we attach to them. And if you're not talking about inequality, then boosting social mobility is sort of meaningless.'

In the end, social mobility was worth it for me. Some discomfort in exchange for increased opportunity is a good deal providing your sense of self remains intact. It shouldn't be one of the few ways to guarantee decent pay and working conditions, though. It's also OK to change a bit – we all adapt to new environments and experiences – but it shouldn't be a requirement or expectation that you completely transform. Social mobility shouldn't be a finishing school for poor people.

No amount of straightened hair, shiny suits, voice changing, tap dancing, pulling-up-your pants or taking-your-hoodie-off-and-hustling is going to make anyone worth your time like or respect you. No one should feel shame because they don't have enough money to live comfortably, that there is worry and panic when the fridge breaks or the car gives in. Do not waste your life 'breaking stereotypes' to prove your worth. Play the game as much as is necessary to get the things that you want. Suppress your anger in the short term to avoid getting fired. Code-switch to secure that promotion. Then if you ascend to a position of power, stop perpetuating these imaginary markers of talent, decorum and success.

And if you can, don't internalise them.

• • •

I wouldn't change a thing about the experiences that have shaped me. But I miss people saying what they mean and saying it directly. Instead, I spend my days sending passive aggressive emails that are performatively polite in the name of 'professionalism'.* I'm sad that there are parts of black culture that will never be mine. For every art gallery or workplace that I glide through, there's a nightclub, a phrase, a shared look, that isn't mine to own, although I wish it were. And if you ever see me doing a full shop at a Waitrose, please send me back to my mum's. I've decided some dogs are OK.

I don't miss the threat of bailiffs, hire purchasing everything, putting the meter on emergency or getting stuck in the lift with a fucking pitbull that's done a piss in it. I still like landfill indie music. It's nice to have a garden.

But I hate that I like *Blackadder*.

---

* You can't say, 'I sent you that already,' you have to say, 'As per my last email,' before passive aggressively repeating the information you sent the week before.

3 Dispatches from my gap year travel diary: part one, aged nineteen

21 February 2010 – Paraty, Brazil

We've met some people from Wellington College* [min. £10,380 per term] in our year which is so random.

The guy who was constantly attached to a spliff said that their [sic] was much more community when it was run by drug lords.

3 March – eighteen-hour bus

The views from the bus our [sic] pretty incredible but not as incredible as our drunken karaoke and dancing, with personal favourites being Journey and my performance of 'Bad Romance' with dance routine . . . twice.

9 March – five-hour bus to Corrientes

We were all under the impression he was our age or perhaps just finished uni when he was in fact about twenty-five.

I feel like Che Guevara but with a language barrier instead of a motorcycle.

* A super fancy private school in Berkshire, so fancy it's called a public school.

20th March – end of Buenos Aires ☹

As much as I hate colonialism, they sure knew how to make an excellent building!

There were banners stating 'Las Malvinas [the Falkland Islands] sera y seran Argentinas' so we pretended to be Americans.

28 March – rest day

Adam got me a Reading Festival ticket!!! I do miss my gay best friend. It's weird not having Frankie, Claire & Susie to obsess over things and admire Gaga and Beyoncé.

31 March – Porterillos

The village is small and very spread out with no internet. This means three days on we still don't know the Reading Festival line-up!

We have been in the country[side] for far too long, and although it is beautiful here I am not a nature lover and miss the internet.

4 April – back from Porterillos

I decided to go to bed. Not before, however, trying to explain to my dance partner what a 'Sexy Bitch' was. After hearing the Akon song he kept asking 'What is it, what is a Sexy Bitch?' and we tried to explain but it was too hard and too funny!

13 April – super nice bus to Salta

We also met the coolest couple from London, a French girl who worked for the BFI and a guy who worked for the civil service. I hope to be as cool as them when I'm thirty.

22 Abril [April in Spanish] – Salt flat tour complete!

Politics is a constant topic of conversation for us and Dave & Dave seemed to find my hatred of David Cameron quite funny and in return Google Imaged pictures of their PM who was extremely unattractive.

29 April' – Cochabamba

I had a fantastic Larium [malaria tablets] induced dream in which I was in a hot tub with the Arctic Monkeys, and Alex Turner's hair was still cute and he was in love with me.

On a toilet stop in a random village, a girl saw me, stared, ran to her friend in shock and pointed at me in an annoying and rude manner. They clearly didn't have MTV and hadn't seen a black person before.

12 May – La Paz

We were put on the waiting list along with Benedict. I could smell the private education and his Warwick course. He said sweeping statements that pained me about the north, the class system and race that we hadn't quite known each other long enough for.

21 May – back in Cusco, Eli's b'day

The walk down the mountain gave me awful blisters. My blisters angered me and I swore a lot and kicked stones to release my fury.

13 July – home for twelve days

I cried when I saw my parents but now it's like I never left.

4 The right kind of family

She wishes they could see her now. She's wearing tailored trousers, a silk blouse, wedge heels. She's applied makeup, hidden her puffy eyelids behind thick tortoiseshell frames. The police officers and social worker should have seen her like this, competent and refined and trustworthy. The judge will see that she's not an alcoholic, not an addict, that she has no criminal record. She has bachelor's and master's degrees in literature from Brown and Columbia.[1]

Frida's internal monologue in Jessamine Chan's *The School for Good Mothers* (2022)

My mom, well, after we talked about everything, she was like, "The one thing I learned raising you – through successes and failures – is that the best way to be a mother is to do so with as many other moms around as possible." You laid out a number of options for me to choose from, and the thing is, honestly – what if we had them all?[2]

Katrina speaking to Ames in Torrey Peters' *Detransition, Baby* (2021)

When I was seventeen I got very sick. It was 2008 and Mum went on holiday for a week. This was the first break she'd had in five years and if anyone deserved it, she did. She had been the main carer for my gran, Daphne, as she died of cancer. As the bad cells multiplied, metastasising from the breasts to the lungs, the tasks Mum took on grew too. Every modicum of independence Gran lost, Mum gained as care work as well as grief. So when I too got sick while she was away and started to lose control of my body, my teenage logic decided it was best not to ruin this holiday for her with a new worry.

I spent the week Mum was away boarding at school. Every night, my bed was covered in an ocean of sweat. In the early afternoon, I kept sleeping for hours at a time and would wake up disorientated and alarmed. I'd been taking a laxative for my bunged-up stomach but it wasn't working. My stomach was distended, slowly ballooning in size as my appetite plummeted. I'd been so looking forward to eating a full English every morning at school, stacking the hash browns into towers only to demolish them, but I could only hold down juice and tea. If I hadn't been a virgin, I would have worried I was pregnant. When in the corridor a teacher said that I looked pregnant, I burst into tears. Would I, Kimberly McIntosh, scholar since age seven, a clean sweep of As at GCSE, a virgin, and even back then, a believer in abortion, allow myself to get and stay pregnant? 'I'm sick,' I told her outside assembly. 'And I don't know what's wrong with me.' Being thought of as pregnant was more distressing to me than my undiagnosed illness.

The GP who had seen me for what we had believed to be constipation sent me straight to A&E to get an emergency suite of scans; ultrasound, CT, MRI. I look young for my age, so when I rocked up, a black teenager with her early twenties cousin (who'd given me a lift), no parents in sight and, to top it off, looking pregnant, I was in the cross-fire of assumptions. I wasn't treated as a minor, but an imposition.

'You can't just come here without an appointment asking for

scans!!!' a nurse screamed at me after two hours spent sitting on an uncomfortable plastic chair. She gave me an appointment in three weeks' time and I went back to school. I'd be back a few days later anyway, as an emergency in-patient, first with my uncle, then with my parents. As we sat in the ultrasound lounge with all the pregnant women, Mum would catch their quick glances, sorrowful and judgemental. So she spoke loudly on the phone to a relative, making sure to denote how scary it was that I had an unspecified disease, and WAS NOT PREGNANT.

Once it was established that I was telling the truth about my virginity, I went from object of disdain to object of pity and intrigue. I was a puzzle for the doctors to solve and a lesson for the juniors. I wasn't part of a 'dysfunctional', absent family but an overbearing, hyper-present one demanding updates. I certainly benefitted from Dad's middle classness – that understated, passive aggressive belligerence, that 'can I speak to the manager' muted fury while I waited for a diagnosis. When senior doctors saw my dad in the corridor they would swivel in the opposite direction and speedwalk away from him to escape further haranguing until I was diagnosed with non-pulmonary tuberculosis.

In retrospect, respectability politics put my health at risk but also saved my life. It got me dismissed from A&E when I needed a diagnosis. But I only went back to the GP, triggering that chain of events, out of shame. I couldn't think of anything worse than being branded as an unmarried, black, young mum, even hypothetically. This wasn't the type of motherhood I was meant to aspire to. Looking after children is known to be hard, so going it alone, especially at a young age, is difficult and calls for significant sacrifice whether that be money or leisure time. It was a destiny I was meant to avoid because it's a stereotype I was to subvert at all costs. Yet this describes some of my family members who are fantastic mothers.

Black people, and particularly black women, can't make choices about childbearing, partnership or marriage without those decisions being understood, by some, to be political problems.[3] It is why the very real statistic – that black women are twice as likely to be single parents than the England and Wales average[4] – is weighted with unspoken baggage. These stats are true for black women with Caribbean and African heritage (these are Census categories – not mine – I know Africa and the Caribbean are not countries). And it's because these categories encompass so many different countries, cultures, histories, migration patterns and ideas about family that I focus mostly on the Caribbean, where my heritage lies. But because of how we are racialised in Britain, the narratives about black families and partnership affect a lot of us regardless of where our parents or grandparents were born.

After the Second World War, the welfare state in the UK entrenched an already existing orthodoxy that a nuclear family of a wage-earning husband and homemaking wife with biological children was the norm.[5] This 'ideal' family was to be a refuge from the world of work for men and a hub of emotional support and care for husbands and children. Women were responsible for providing this care and encouraged to prioritise the physical and psychological well-being of others above themselves. Anything that deviated from this was often pathologised.[6]

Today, there is much greater acceptance and recognition of the myriad ways we make families. The 2018 British Social Attitudes survey for that year revealed that only 16 per cent of people were against a couple with young children divorcing. Only 12 per cent disapproved of living together with children while not being married. Over the past thirty years, 'let people live' has increasingly become the vibe as views on people's relationships and lifestyles have loosened. The idea that a family should consist of a married heterosexual couple with children has been challenged. The rising proportion of women in paid work, the normalisation of divorce, the growth of single parenthood and co-parenting, the legalisation of same-sex marriage, the increasing number of single people living alone, and the growing number of people who are not having children, have widened the boundaries of what counts as a 'legitimate' life.[7] Views on families have relaxed, but not for everyone. If you're part of an 'out-group', say on a low income, queer, an ethnic minority or a combination, adhering to cultural norms like getting married can be a gateway to greater acceptance and respect.

'Now don't you become someone's baby mother! You're better than that!' the father of Candice Brathwaite, influencer and author of *I Am Not Your Baby Mother*, warned her. 'Try and get married first,' her aunties advised. 'It just sets a better *tone*.'[8] I have heard the same overtures touted not only as a ticket to community respect (almost always directed at black women and not at men) but also as a solution to poverty and a way to improve educational attainment. These beliefs start to leak into government policy, how social services are delivered and programmes run by charities.

These ideas about marriage and family shaped my dreams and aspirations in my teens. I spent a lot of my childhood and teens in my head building intricate, detailed and delusional fantasies of my future life. That future always included an illustrious career and a rich but otherwise formless husband. I would live in an attractive detached home with a garage and a winding drive and push one of those bulbous and cumbersome Silver Cross prams. To this day, I absent-mindedly doodle detached houses with a garage on the side onto meeting agendas and scrap paper. I could waste half an hour designing elaborate weddings in my head that were held in the make-believe equivalent of the Palace of Versailles.

Life as an adult doesn't resemble the fantasies of adolescence. My twenties were more turbulent than the one I imagined. Real life was more complicated. The realities of relationships both platonic and romantic were trickier than I had thought they would be but also more rewarding. Friendships, not romance, played the starring role and were my primary source of social support. And the resurgence of popular feminism in the 2010s coincided with my coming-of-age. I started to question whether the configuration of my desires were things I actually wanted or if I was drunk on the discourse of what a perfect life should be. I know there is social capital that comes with conformity. It's not just that inquisitive relatives will let you rest at Christmas if you're in a long-term relationship or engaged, or that it would make your mum happy. It's also that the personal lives of single people are not taken as seriously as those of couples. It is the external validation that marriage and children bring (which are not good reasons to do either of those things).

In 2022, the Office of National Statistics (ONS) released the latest data on childbearing and found that half of women born in 1990 were still 'childless' by their thirtieth birthday (the highest on record).[9] I am one of them and I feel ambivalent about having children. When my first female friend had a baby, I didn't feel the pang of want or longing I'd read about. I did feel disorientated by the passage of time, which had moved languidly in our teens and had somehow sped up without me noticing. Our lives had been intertwined for so long and somewhere in the web of that fifteen years of laughing and dancing and decisions big and small a new life had begun. I was moved by it, but it didn't awaken any dormant maternal hunger in me.

I am not alone in this but it's a mixed assortment of feelings. Some of my friends are objectively happy with their lives as they are but know they want a family and haven't met a partner yet. This pains them in the same way a bruise does – they only remember if someone pokes it purposefully or hits them by accident with a comment or a phrase. Every date or party with strangers in attendance becomes freighted with possibility. There are friends who do not see children in their future. It's not a long-standing conviction they've had since childhood. It's a slow realisation that has grown steadily as their sense of self stabilised and matured. Then there are the friends who feel the same as me. We could go either way, stuck in a purgatory of indecision. Plus as one friend put it: 'With what money????' The UK has some of the highest childcare costs in Europe.[10]

Some of my doubt is driven by the weight of caring responsibilities and my fear of it. Between 2021 and 2022, the number of women not working to look after family rose by 5 per cent, the first sustained increase in at least thirty years. The sharpest rise was for women aged twenty-five to thirty-four.[11] Among heterosexual couples, it's still women who do most of the caring and housework. This isn't just a personal choice – public policy is based on the assumption that they will (or that they can afford to pay someone, usually a migrant woman, to help). It's the meagre paternity leave on offer and the gender pay gaps that force a division of labour on straight couples they don't necessarily want. In reality, caring for people is hard work, a multitude of joys and burdens.[12] But women are meant to be driven to care not by duty, obligation or expectation, but by 'unconditional love' and to give it without complaint. This may sound like an exaggeration or a way of thinking we've long moved past. It's not. Whether it's an article about a woman being child-free by choice, or a nuanced take on the realities of motherhood, harsh critique is never far behind.[13]

Knowing this, I've become more interested in other ways to live, especially after turning thirty. In a society that still prioritises the nuclear family and judges people who don't conform, how can I drown out the din of societal expectations and, in the quiet, hear my true desires instead?

• • •

When I was twenty-six my date asked me if I knew my dad as he knew this was a 'problem' in my community (the black community btw, if that's not clear!*). It was 2017 and I was in a nondescript restaurant in the City, London's sterile financial district famous for its characterless bars. I would like to say that I gave an impassioned lecture about the legacies of slavery and stereotypes, got

* And yes he is—

up and left – but that would be a lie. I told him that my dad, like many dads, works in IT. He also runs a small charity in his spare time and lives with his new wife and children. If anything, Dad's transgressions bore me because they are so conventional. The mundanity of several adulteries followed by a messy divorce and, in an attempt to save face, pretending it never happened and seeking refuge in respectability. If private school was anything to go by, this was not a turn of events exclusive to black families. People are messy and nothing is messier than family.

The following year, my Twitter timeline was ablaze with outrage. Photos of a textbook littered with stereotypes made its way onto Facebook before cross-pollinating onto Twitter.[14] An AQA GCSE Sociology textbook published by Hodder Education claimed that 'working-class children often lack the appropriate attitudes, norms and values that are necessary to succeed in education' and 'the typical Chinese family is a strongly patriarchal arrangement based on the three rules of obedience: a daughter obeys her father, a married woman obeys her husband, a widow obeys her son'.[15]

But it was the section describing Caribbean fathers as 'largely absent' with children commonly 'passed between relatives' that initially sparked the backlash. After coverage in the *Huffington Post* and on *BBC Newsbeat*, Hodder reviewed the textbook and the offending pages were removed.[16] In a follow-up piece by the reporter Nadine White, then at the *Huffington Post*, the first post in the comment section posits: 'But were they [the textbook authors] factually wrong?'[17]

It's true that different cultures and countries and communities have different ways of building families and parenting. The history of the nuclear family in England is a contested one. Historians and sociologists disagree on when it started and its prevalence.[18] What is clear is that during the twentieth century, there was a move away from extended families and into more separate, nuclear ones.[19] To this day, this model is reinforced by popular media, particularly by advertising. By understanding and shaping our aspirations, adverts sell us products, services and experiences. And although there has been increased diversity (like more same-sex couples and black people), it is still normally within the confines of a two-parent family with one or two children. When the family is black, they are usually middle-class, lighter-skinned or one of the partners is white (normally a white man and a black woman).[20] Marketing depicts images of a 'good' and 'desirable' life and the nuclear family of two different-sex partners continues to dominate.[21]

This limited view of family is perceived as universal and projected onto other societies and cultures. This doesn't always make sense, like trying to square a circle and blaming the circle when it's found impossible. One-size-fits-all works best for the people of average weight and height. Everyone else is left drowning or trying to squeeze into something not designed with them in mind.[22] Some of the pushback against the Sociology textbook wasn't about the statements themselves. It was that they were standalone. There was no research, no citations, no history to accompany them and give them context. 'Our failure to conform to western notions of the (nuclear) family is not seen as a legacy of slavery, when marriage was actively discouraged [or] other alternative models of marriage and family life,' wrote Beverly Bryan, Stella Dadzie and Suzanne Scafe, the academics and organisers in *Heart of the Race: Black Women's Lives in Britain*. 'Instead it is blamed on promiscuity, our irresponsibility and our general lack of moral fibre as a people.'[23]

These judgements are bad in and of themselves. But these beliefs can influence the way people behave, including those working in public services. One such judgement was given on an afternoon in the late seventies, when my mum was walking with her two nephews, my eldest cousins, through Reading town centre. She was babysitting them so that my aunty could go to work. By the traffic light crossing where Broad Street meets West Street, Mum spotted one of her old teachers, Mrs Dubois.

'Hello, Mrs Dubois!' She waved. Mrs Dubois looked down at the two young children and then back at the sixteen-year-old holding their hands.

'I knew it! I knew it!' she said with an air of disgust and an unfounded, prophetic certainty. 'I knew this is what you would do.' This wasn't a scenario that triggered Mrs Dubois' concern. She didn't toy with involving social services to help a minor, who she believed already had two children. This was Mum's destiny.

'I was shouting that they weren't mine!' Mum said. 'But it was like I was speaking another language. Like she couldn't hear me.'

But these stereotypes aren't new, they're steeped in history. In 1939, the West India Royal Commission, a government investigation into the causes of the labour protests across the Caribbean, noted a number of 'defects' in families. These included statements that 'unscrupulous and improvident father evad[ing] his children and probably [their] unmarried mother' and 'obsessive mother–son relationships' were leaving Caribbean people incapable of maintaining satisfactory relationships with each other.[24] This was followed by colonial anthropologists from the UK, whose studies in the 1940s to 1960s observed 'defective and deviant' families that didn't model themselves on the 'norm' of the middle-class, middle-England, nuclear family. Fathers were characterised as absent and promiscuous and women as having a 'problematically' dominant role in the household that marginalised men.[25]

In reality, there are a range of family patterns in the Caribbean, and they differ between islands and across class lines. A single-parent family, headed by the mum, is a feature of family life in the Caribbean, a pattern that emerged during slavery because patterns often outlast the conditions that led to their creation. In Jamaica, it's more common for working-class people to live in a household where the male partner doesn't live in the house on a permanent basis but is still considered part of the family and regularly visits. In Antigua and Barbados, a married two-parent family is more prevalent than in Jamaica.[26] People's lives aren't static, they also move through different types of relationships throughout their lives: single, living together, marriage, a new relationship.

The prominence of Christianity in Jamaica also meant that the institution of marriage was still an aspiration for many. That being said, the precarious nature of employment was not only a reason for migrating in the first place, but also made it more common to wait until later in life to marry, after years of independence and former relationships.[27] While waiting for the economic stability necessary for the ceremony, it was ordinary to live with your significant other in a 'common law' marriage until the time was right.[28]

It was also common for parents to leave the Caribbean for the UK in search of work and leave their children in the care of extended family until they could save for their passage. This could take a decade and became part of the family structure.[29] Research from the time estimated that between 96 and 98 per cent of Jamaican migrants to Britain left their children behind.[30] This was true in my family, where three of my aunts waited for nearly a decade in Jamaica until my gran had the fare to send for them. They lived with their aunt and then quite abruptly were told they were moving to England to meet a person who, to them, was a stranger who sent letters and presents.

That these family patterns would replicate themselves when people migrated to the UK from the 1950s shouldn't be surprising. Instead, it's been a remarkably agile moral panic, held responsible for the 1981 Brixton riots, educational underachievement of black Caribbean boys, knife and gun crime, and black boys not being . . . 'manly' enough.

In a 2010 *Guardian* article titled, 'Black boys are too feminised', Dr Tony Sewell, the founder of the charity *Generating Genius*,* wrote that, more than racism, 'the main problem holding back black boys academically is their over-feminised upbringing'. He

* Before someone drags me, I interviewed Tony Sewell for my master's thesis before I knew this. I just thought he was a dude with a charity!

said his educational summer camp for black boys 'freed them from the arms of their single mothers' (as if it were a prison) before warning that 'the black family continues to disintegrate and it seems no one dares say a word'.[31] These views clearly influenced the direction of the widely discredited 2021 Commission on Race and Ethnic Disparities, which he chaired. The *Guardian* journalist Aditya Chakrabortty saw an email the commission sent to two leading academics fishing for evidence 'to support perceptions that young people living in single-parent households' are more likely to become involved in crime.[32] They didn't find any.

Contrary to Sewell's claim that no one's talking about black families, people actually have a lot to say, and they are saying it loudly. Interviewing black single mums and dads who lived outside the home, Tracey Reynolds, Professor in the Faculty of Liberal Arts and Sciences at the University of Greenwich, heard from parents who had internalised the negative stereotypes about themselves and the community. The spectre of nineties media coverage about deadbeat, wotless (worthless) black fathers and headstrong black babymothers who couldn't secure a ring and a good man haunted them. Interviewing black single mums, they spoke highly of the black men in their lives, but negatively about black men in general.[33] The fathers felt they were universally branded as 'bad', because they weren't part of a nuclear unit of mum, dad and child or weren't the main earner, even though they tried their best to be there for their kids and have a relationship with them.[34] The launch of podcasts like the UK-based Dope Black Dads, which started in 2018 to counter negative stereotypes and support black fathers, symbolises how potent and pervasive this narrative still is.[35]

I've seen these ideas out in the wild. At a discussion group run by a black-led charity, I was in the bar area of a hotel near Euston Square in central London, part of a circle of black people with an interest in young black people and education. The conversation was lively. People shared their ideas and info about mentoring programmes they ran. I sipped on a red wine and sank into the lounge chair. Then one of the co-founders, a middle-aged to old black man, said that what we really needed were middle-class values. When I asked him if he could specify what he meant by middle-class values, he mentioned the longevity of his marriage. The only other black woman at the event locked eyes with me in disbelief across the circle. It is easier to settle for simplicity and take comfort in the belief that complex problems have easy answers. But if marriage is the solution to the challenges facing black youth then I've got bad news for the rest of the country: in 2019 marriage rates for opposite-sex couples in England and Wales fell to their lowest on record since 1862.[36]

Growing up, these beliefs gripped my imagination too. Rather cruelly, I declared to my divorced mother at about age fifteen that I 'was going to stay married'. Years later, the moment flashed back to me and I apologised. She told me that kids inadvertently say offensive things to their parents all the time. I'd said much worse. She didn't even remember the moment. Although I can't be certain, I think that I wanted to stay married because I wanted to counter the negative associations given to black single motherhood. The dull, one-dimensional images that don't capture the unique intimacy of these relationships. I knew that being married conferred respect inside and outside of our community. Mum once told me that being divorced even gave her status in some settings because she had 'managed' to get married, as if it were an achievement rather than a celebration of love and commitment.

These narratives cut through to white families too. In interviews with white single mums, researchers at the University of Sussex heard from women who felt shame, a loss of status and respect, because of their 'failure' to win the coveted prize, the ultimate trophy of femininity – a nice man and a nice house. The middle-class mums made great pains to distance themselves from the working-class ones, who they claimed chose to be single mums and not work, whereas they claimed they became single through 'unavoidable' circumstances like divorce or being widowed.[37]

'I come from an intelligent circle and then in the wider society there's *Jeremy Kyle*,' white single mum Jess, thirty-nine, told the researchers. 'You're almost up there for the pillory, aren't you? Then you see *Jeremy Kyle* and there are multi-coloured families and stuff. It's sad, it's just like cats having kittens and they have kittens and they keep on having kittens.'[38] She wasn't a babymother or a working-class white woman with a good-for-nothing black babyfather. And she wanted people to know it.

There is nothing shameful about raising a family in whichever way makes sense to you, as long as it isn't causing active harm. Relationships break down and people co-parent. Others decide from the outset to have children without a partner. But I'm not in the business of making excuses for abdicating responsibility. Recognising the complexity and nuance of unflattering and unfair narratives about black families is not a get-out-of-jail-free card for men who leave women to raise children alone, assuming she'll get on with it because that's what women do. It's not an accident that 91 per cent of single parents are women. Women are more likely to take on the main caring responsibilities for children when relationships break down.[39] And just because a male partner lives in the home doesn't mean they're pulling their weight. In 2016, women on average carried out 60 per cent more unpaid work than men, like cooking, cleaning, childcare and other housework.[40] During the first Covid-19 lockdown of 2020, a survey by the Office for National Statistics (ONS) found that women carried out significantly more daily childcare duties than men during lockdown, which negatively affected their mental health.[41]

Looking after children and adults, the physical care of others, is work: challenging yet rewarding, enthralling but sometimes lonely. It's essential work. And it would be much easier if it were shared with as many people as possible and our public services made it easy to do that.

• • •

'It's a sort of, like, an African thing. That it takes a village to raise a family,' Laura, a foster parent with Caribbean heritage, told me. After fifteen years working in schools, she was driving home and she saw three adverts calling for more foster carers. 'I grew [up] in a one-parent house. And my dad, he just did everything. I always thought about giving back because of what my dad did. And then my kids, I was always helping their mates.'

In England, about 45,370 families are fostering 57,380 children.[42] Over the past twenty years, some of those kids have come through our door back home in Reading to live with my mum and some of them are still there.

Like most teenagers, I wanted to be as normal as possible. Conformity was king, although small flourishes of individuality were allowed so you seemed a bit interesting. I had a phase of wearing a tie to school because it *wasn't* a prescribed part of the girls' uniform, borrowed from a friend's older brother. I developed an aggressive addiction to headbands, at first as a way to hide relaxer regrowth, which soon became a personality trait. Fostering was the opposite of conformity, it screamed different. If 'normal' is two straight, married parents, who love their kids unconditionally and raise them in perfect harmony, then fostering at first glance is its opposite and I resented that.

If for whatever reason you can't be raised by a biological family member, the council will become involved in your care. This disrupts so much of what people assume when they hear the word family: that we can't choose them, that blood is thicker than water, and that parents own their children and have the final say on what they're allowed to do and what happens to them. When it works, fostering cultivates families' best traits and proves that it can be more expansive than what we're sold and can transcend the artificial boundaries of blood ties: generosity, empathy, extending yourself to nurture people you care about.

Wilma has been fostering for six years and her biological children are very involved with her two long-term foster children:

'They go cycling, they'll go to the park together. These girls are actually part of the family.' Natalie's biological daughter and son-in-law regularly visit her foster daughter at university. 'They see her often, which is good. She calls them [sic] Aunty. She's very, very close to them.'

Fostering also shows us how stereotypes, assumptions and judgements about families can harm the very people they're meant to help. My mum was (incorrectly) judged by her former teacher in the street, who assumed she was an underage mother of two and did not see that as a safeguarding concern. But at least at that point she had no power over her life (although she certainly did before). I was judged in the hospital when no one would help me because they thought I was a pregnant teenager. But I had the resources to quickly bypass the gatekeepers and soon had the diagnosis and treatment I needed. This lack of compassion from services whose mission is supposedly to care for us has a much bigger impact on other people who are at the sharp end of their decisions and who do not have the means, by luck or circumstance, to circumvent them.

In their study of social workers in deprived areas in England, Professor Paul Bywater and his colleagues saw social workers with increasing caseloads and beholden to a risk-averse culture. Understandably, when children's safety is on the line, staff want to err on the side of caution.[43] At times, this turned into a punitive approach that blamed the families they worked with for things outside of their control, like living in a deprived area or being poor.[44] Another study by Bywater uncovered a complex reality where ethnicity, deprivation and the part of town you live in all affect the chance your child could end up in care.*

'People judge families through a white *and* middle-class lens,' Beverly Jones, Associate Director for Practice and Impact at the

* Lower Super Outputs Areas (LSOAs) in England and Wales or their equivalents in the other countries. LSOAs are small neighbourhoods of approximately 1,600 people on average.

Family Justice Observatory, tells the journalist Polly Curtis in her book, *Behind Closed Doors: Why We Break Up Families – and How to Mend Them*. This can lead to unconscious misunderstandings and outright racism, both with serious implications.[45]

When my mum was applying to be a foster carer, the social worker told her she was concerned that she was isolating herself, because her front blinds were always closed, which was apparently a cause of concern. Mum had to explain that it's because lots of people of Caribbean heritage don't like random people being able to look into their living rooms and know all their business. Her mum did it, and now she did it too. It would have otherwise gone down as a mark against her. Valerie, a foster carer for five years, found her offer to look after her foster child long term blocked by her family finder. She believes this is because of her race. The child is white and she is black. 'Get him into a nice little English family,' she told me. She said that 148 families visited the child and said his care needs were too complicated. 'Even though I said to them, I would take him on. The lady who was the family finder wasn't keen on him being with me because of my colour. And that's the truth. I said he's in his forever home already. But she couldn't see that. She didn't want that for him.'

After two years of back-and-forth, things sped up when Valerie got a new family finder. She could see how much she cared for the child and ended the search for a 'nice, white family'. Cultural matching, where social services work hard to place children with families that are culturally similar, is important. It's particularly urgent for ethnic minority children who will form their identities in a country where they are not the majority. The issue, the carers told me, is that there is a double standard. 'I found that whenever they were black [children] going to [a] white [family] or even white adopting white – it went through real fast, really, really fast.'

Acknowledging race in fostering and adoption is critical, as Annalisa Toccara, co-director of Adoptee Futures, knows: 'I think if we are going to adopt, then as much as possible, we need to be able to keep a child's culture alive. My birth dad requested that I was placed with black Jamaican parents, he specifically said that,' she told me. Annalisa and I met serendipitously. In 2018, she organised a panel with *gal-dem*, a zine dedicated to platforming the voices of women and non-binary people of colour, on sexual harassment for the Sheffield Festival of Debate. She recognised me from her family WhatsApp. Her adoptive father is related to my father. My dad had posted a video of me on Sky News talking about the Windrush scandal in the group chat, and she told me she was pretty sure we were related, although not by blood. In 2019, a year after we first met, she spoke to Metro.co.uk about her adoption. She told them that while her heritage was actively affirmed in the home, this wasn't always reflected in the wider world. Annalisa was adopted when she was four years old and identifies as both black and mixed-heritage.[46] 'When we look at transracially adopted* kids, they turn into adults who potentially might not know about their background or their history, and then they're having to discover that through, for example, Ancestry DNA,' she told me. In a bid to find out about their heritage, adoptees were resorting to genome testing services to find out about their ancestry, for example 23andMe.

Black children fostered and adopted by non-black families risk not being celebrated anywhere. In a report by the Black Care Experience, adults who had been fostered and adopted by non-black families reported racist comments from carers, a lack of connection with their heritage as the carers had no interest, having their hair cut off or damaged with relaxers that went wrong, and dry skin and eczema issues.[47] But while Annalisa's adoption was a successful cultural match and her life is brimming with traditional markers of success – a loving upbringing, a master's degree with a PhD on the way, a book on adoption in the works,

* Transracial or interracial adoption describes any situation in which a family adopts a child of a different race.

and her own charitable organisation – she's struggled with elements of her adoption. 'The article [on Metro.co.uk], that really started my brains thinking a bit more about it,' she said. Through the community she built, Adoptee Futures, she has connected with others who feel the same way. 'A lot of the marketing campaigns for adoption recruitment really portray this idealistic experience of what adoption is. I know, from my experience, it's not like that. And I also know that from talking to other adoptees. It doesn't quite match up.'

The notion that adoption is a selfless, beautiful act that saves children and gives them their happy ever after is damaging for children and parents (biological and adoptive) alike.[48] It can make it difficult for adoptees to raise legitimate questions about the past or acknowledge pain during difficult days, such as birthdays, for fear of upsetting their adoptive parents. 'I had a great upbringing. But I've had mental health issues since I was nineteen. My attachment issues with relationships, with friends. I don't have secure attachments at all,' Annalisa said. 'I think that if [my parents] had had proper education around how the trauma of adoption can affect a child, then maybe, actually that would have helped them to not blame themselves. At the same time, we would then be able to understand ourselves more and why we behave the way we do.'

In 2021, 2,870 children were adopted.[49] Adoption has been promoted by government policy in England in recent years as the best solution for children from vulnerable families.

The UK is one of the few countries in Europe that allow non-consensual adoptions – where children are adopted against the wishes of their birth parents.[50] One foster carer told me that her foster children were being pushed for adoption when they were aged two and four. The carer told their social workers not to pursue this, as the children still loved their parents and 'talked about them every day'. Luckily, social services listened and they remained in long-term foster care and have contact with their birth family as appropriate.

At the time of writing, there is no legal requirement for adoptive families to maintain contact of any kind with their child's birth family once an adoption order has gone through.[51] In 2017, the senior judge Lord Justice McFarlane argued that too many children were being forcibly adopted against the wishes of their families and prevented from having any contact with their birth parents.[52] Annalisa wonders why we're trying to eradicate birth families: 'We're trying to make adoptive parents feel better. That's all it is.' The cookie-cutter image of family as a unit encourages some adopters to sever adoptees biological ties, so the family they've created more closely matches the 'norm'. Speaking to Annalisa has pushed me to think much more critically about adoption, which previously I'd considered as an alternative to having biological children if I decided later on that that was something I wanted. Fostering and adoption are not forms of insurance against my ambivalence and uncertainty about procreation and declining fertility. It's signing up for a specific type of care that most likely involves trauma. People should go into it because they think they can give that, not as a back-up plan.

• • •

'It's not a job. It's a way of life' is a phrase I heard again and again from the foster carers I spoke to about how they understand their unique role in a system that makes them both carers and workers. The International Labour Organization states that care work is the job of looking after the physical, psychological, emotional and developmental needs of one or more other people.[53] Lots of care work is paid (although not enough). Nurseries, childminders, care homes for elderly people, supported accommodation, hospitals and schools are all places where this happens. Without it our society and economy can't function.

But the relationship between a parent and a child is not like that between a child and a teacher or nursery worker. It's the social bond most heavily weighted with obligation and responsibility. Reneging on it receives the utmost social sanction. When a woman named Victoria Elder posted on the question-and-answer site Quora that she regretted becoming a mother she was bombarded by furious replies calling her self-centred, insecure and in need of therapy. There were also messages of praise for her honesty.[54]

Foster care dissolves the boundaries between public and private and brings the sanctimony of love for children, and the altruism, sacrifice and devotion (from women) that it demands, in crash collision with workers' rights.

To me, fostering gives life to the feminist demand that 'care work is work' and deserves to be paid. One carer, Sarah, told me she's worked with two separate fathers who tried to kill their babies by throwing them against a wall. Biological parents finding out where you live and threatening you as a way to feel some control when they feel powerless was mentioned more than once. Having the skills to involve them in the lives of their children in small, safe ways is a crucial part of the job. Wilma, having fostered for six years, likened it to being a detective. 'Some of [the children] have been through such a lot of trauma, and often undiscovered trauma. These traumas are live,' she told me. 'I have to be present to how they're going to respond to it emotionally. Being a detective, but also being this mothering, caring sort of person.'

But children should never feel like commodities. Annalisa feels the adoption system can make children feel like products to be purchased. 'There was an interesting tweet a couple of weeks ago. It was these two adopted children in the UK, who had a barcode as a tattoo. There was, like, a family joke,' she said. And although the fees paid to foster carers aren't particularly high for twenty-four-hour care, it brings a transactional element to it. When Sarah first applied to be a foster carer, she was told: 'The wages are low, the work is hard.' But anything that is marketised runs the risk of people doing it for the money. 'You got carers and carers: carers that really care and carers that are there for the money,' Valerie, a foster carer of five years, said. 'There's a load of them in the system here. I'll tell you – a lot of them. They're just reaping the money but don't give a damn about the children.' Discouraging people like this from becoming carers would take reform of the care system but also the economy. It will only become less attractive if there are alternative ways for people to make a decent living.

I don't see a wage and care as incompatible. Social security supports people with the costs of raising a child or caring for loved ones, although it is nowhere near enough. Feminist campaigns like Wages for Housework aren't about making everything we do transactional. They're about making the work of looking after people visible and valued (which in a capitalist society is linked to pay and prestige), until we've built a better alternative.[55] Care without love and compassion is a problem, though.

We have government-run (and outsourced) services that are underfunded. It has made them gutted and fragile and it's hard for the staff who work in them to steady themselves. Dominant ideas of what a family should look like are not only outdated and limiting, making people feel like failures when they don't conform, they also shape how these services are delivered, with sometimes disastrous consequences. These ideas can leave people with limited support networks and insurmountable responsibilities.

In the afterword of her novel *Careless*, author Kirsty Capes explains what she wanted the protagonist Bess to tell readers: 'What she shows us – and what care-experienced women understand to be true – is that the mythologisation of biological supremacy in motherhood negates and undermines the other kinds of motherhood that are just as joyous, just as essential, and just as perfect.'[56] This can come from anyone in our lives.

I felt viscerally that families are made when I attended my great-uncle's funeral and at his wife's funeral months later. They had long, full lives. They had lived and taught in schools in Jamaica and London. Fond memories from old pupils on both sides of the Atlantic were read out to the congregation and invited tears.

They didn't have children of their own but the role they had played in the lives of other people's children laced the eulogies. They helped new Caribbean migrants settle and navigate the cold weather and cold public reception. That is what family is, and that is what care is, to me.

Speaking to Annalisa pushed me to re-evaluate my ideas about family and blood ties. We do not owe anyone a relationship simply because we're biologically related to them. But understanding who we are matters. People deserve to know their history and their story and should have the autonomy to decide the role that plays in their lives, as long as it's safe to do so. Our conversation made me acknowledge that trauma shapes many of our relationships with other people, including our families, whatever they look like. Being at those two funerals personified biology's limits. Most people there were from my dad's side of the family and I'm not close to many of them. I have siblings from his second marriage who I think are funny, intelligent and thoughtful people on the cusp of adulthood. I loved spending time with them that day and continue to. I want them in my life. But they don't feel like family in the way, say, my maternal cousins do because I grew up with them. They babysat me, mocked me, and pulled out the controller from the PlayStation so I didn't ruin the game for them. I don't find this upsetting. I find it liberating. It represents possibilities, the possibility that families are what you make them.

I don't know what I want my future family to look like. I have no idea whether I want to get married. I don't know if I want children. If I do, I need to do it my way and because I want to, not out of a fear of being read as incomplete, a failure or being left behind. I don't necessarily need a partnership, but I'd definitely need a community. There is no one clear vision of the future that I desire (although if someone asked what I aspire to right now it would be Clara Amfo energy: a black woman with a great career, impeccable outfits, and, by the looks of it, lots of mates). But knowing that family, that communities, are built, makes me a little less afraid.

5 Dispatches from my gap year travel diary: part two, aged nineteen

14 February 2010

The heat kills my appetite so I should get buff thighs hopefully! ☺

16 February

After washing my hair for the first time without a hairdryer it looks passable, kind of like what my hair usually looks like after I've tried to blow-dry it. My progressive, aka Brazilian, permanent blow-dry is working a treat atm but it's early days.

21 February – Paraty City, Brazil

As Fred, the American at Chill [hostel] explained, dragon slaying is when one guy in a group while out sacrifices himself and gets with the ugly girl of the group so his friends can get with all the hot friends thus 'slaying' the dragon. 'You make her feel special and have the time of her life.' In nightclubs, all over the world for the next decade, I will be in fear that I am being dragon slayed.

3 March – eighteen-hour bus

One of the Danish girls let me use her straighteners and then the English girl straightened it for me, thus proving there is a God.

20 March – end of Buenos Aires ☹

I refrained from buying anything in Zara. I would pick up a hairdryer unable to deal with my hair expanding at rapid speed and the dire need to wash it.

Adverts for *Jersey Shore* have begun and they are quality. This show, with all its controversy and slicked back, wet look hair, is bound to be so horrendous it's brilliant and fun and starts miercoles [Wednesday] at 8 p.m.

It turns out from talking last night that the boys don't know what cellulite is or what it looks like, only that they heard it looks like sausage being squeezed through mesh! After too much curiosity I googled it for Eli, but only on Kate Moss.

6 Is she hot or is she just blonde?

I'm shocked at this strong preference [for Leanne].

Winter *Love Island* 2020 contestant Jess Gale, expressing her surprise that Mike Boateng (who is black) has chosen Leanne Amaning (who is black) over her, a blonde woman with lip fillers.

I've always had a soft spot for 'romance' reality shows. I had a nineties childhood where Cilla Black decided a *Blind Date* contestant's fate. We laughed at them, but in the words of Tyra Banks: we were rooting for them.

Then dating shows became cruel; out to shame and embarrass. Why anyone went on these shows is beyond me. Back then, there were no promises of fast-fashion deals, a pivot to TV presenting, or one million Instagram followers – just a faint chance at love and, likely, humiliation. But sign up they did. So we got the vengeful delight of *Take Me Out*, a guy flying down the 'love lift', lit up in aggressive fluorescent strobes as unforgiving as the contestants. Before this, we were given the unspeakable abomination of *Dating in the Dark*. The premise: singles go on dates in total darkness. They talk, they kiss, they fumble but they cannot see one another. When they are revealed to each other, the lights flick on and we watch them celebrate or recoil.

It's late summer 2009 and I'm lounging on my friend Claire's sofa with our friend Frankie. It's the kind of thoughtless idling that you won't appreciate until it is gone. Twenty-five days' annual leave and bank holidays have no meaning. The long summer breaks feel infinite and unfurl gently, their impermanence not understood. We switch on the TV to watch *Dating in the Dark*. A potential match are on a date, their features blurred into greyish-white shadows on the screen as they laugh at each other's jokes in the infrared light. The date ends and the main light switches on to reveal the most average-looking white man and hottest black woman I've ever seen. She gives him a chance, as they had such a strong 'connection'. But after much deliberation, he rejects her. 'I thought she was blonde,' he says. At first, I'm pained for her, and more acutely pained by what it says about the world I live in. It's swiftly followed by my judgement of the female contestant. Why would she go on a show like this when the rules are different for us?

'I think it is the case . . . for a lot of women, that your first education about how you are perceived racially comes from attraction. You want approval, you want to be seen as attractive, you want to feel desirable. When you're going through adolescence these are the things that preoccupy you,' journalist and broadcaster Afua Hirsch said on the *Growing up with gal-dem* podcast.[1] Discussing an interview she gave to the *Guardian* when she was eighteen, she went on to say: 'If you look at my journey, it started with me trying to understand why I was the only person in my year who didn't have a boyfriend.'

For the racialised but privileged, beauty and desirability might be your first confrontation with racialisation. In school, my teachers had mostly favoured me. I'd never heard of a permanent exclusion, a behaviour management plan or a pupil referral unit. It was easy for me to believe that racism was a thing that bad individuals with backwards beliefs did, rather than a 500-years-and-counting historical process with material consequences.

As a teenager, I didn't think I was ugly, but only adults ever called me beautiful. I was thin, which was imperative in the 'heroin-chic-nothing-tastes-as-good-as-skinny-feels' 2000s, a fashion that as I write is firmly back on trend. But before the resurgence of Y2K, slim-thick 'body positive' candles, Brazilian butt-lift fashion and its demise, there was Trinny and Susannah. I have a big arse that was fortunately celebrated at home, the positive reinforcement able to intercept the messages from Trinny and Susannah's TV show *What Not to Wear*. If a white female contestant ever complained of her 'bum looking big in this', Mum would tell me that 'only white people thought that was bad' and I believed her.

But I wasn't the 'hot' girl and I'd never had a boyfriend. I was often the best friend of a girl everyone wanted. So far, so ordinary. It was not, by any means, a horrible life and I was largely very happy. I had the usual, ubiquitous preoccupations around my appearance and life in general. My flat chest and being short were often on my mind. People even a mere year or two older made me nervous; a year in school life is a chasm of epic proportions.

Then something miraculous happened when I went with my mum to visit her friend, in the London Borough of Newham. It was around 2004 or 2005 and I was thirteen or fourteen. I was reading Nick Hornby's *About a Boy*, which I'd brought with me for the journey. Mum let me hang out with some of the other young people my age, and go for a walk around the estates near where her friend lived, something I was never allowed to do at home where I was consigned to the safety of the inside, stuck writing terrible poetry, reading *Bliss* magazine and downloading songs illegally from LimeWire. The kids tried to explain to me that Dizzee Rascal, and grime in general, was in fact very good, but the memo hadn't reached my school yet. I had also become significantly more desirable in an instant, although my appearance remained unchanged. A mystical spell had been cast upon me; the magic wand of demography. Newham's population was 23 per cent black in 2001.[2] My entire school had maximum ten black people at any one time (a generous estimate). A guy I met that day in East London sent me an email asking me out, which was blocked by my mum who saw this as inappropriate for my age. I returned to Reading and back to the regularly scheduled programming of focusing on my friendships and studies as the source of self-esteem, status and value.

This pattern of desire or 'preferences' followed me into late adolescence and early adulthood. It showed itself, and still does, by the poolside in Jamaican hotels and on the side streets of Peckham, as aunties cajole me into getting my braids redone and the looks of too-old uncles linger on me for too long. Here, I'm the main character, whether I feel like it or not.

'There are no "good" preferences,' the sociologist and essayist Tressie McMillan Cottom writes. 'There are only preferences that are validated by others, differently, based on social contexts.' While at home, McMillan Cottom was immersed in African-American history and culture. But at her racially integrated school in North Carolina she learnt that 'nothing was more beautiful than blond' and that 'there was something powerful about blondness, thinness, flatness, and gaps between thighs. And that power was the context against which all others defined themselves. That was beauty.'[3]

Beauty, attraction and desire feel ethereal. They invoke responses from us that feel outside of our control and are impossible to quantify, unknowable and all-encompassing as a monotheist God. It is a cruel God, because it appears to be bestowed benevolently but without justice, and is swiftly taken away with 'age'. 'Attraction is enormously complex. Sociology comes into play, culture comes into play, our learned behaviours come into play,' Professor of Psychology Dr David Perrett says.[4] We know attraction is complicated and beauty is subjective, hence the ubiquity of the phrase 'Beauty is in the eye of the beholder'. There is even a term for when someone gets more attractive the more you get to know them or has a beauty only you can see: *positive illusions*.[5] We can also find people beautiful but not fancy them at all. There are facial traits that people across cultures rate as attractive (although not the ideal body weight, which is culturally specific).[6] But as Amia Srinivasan, writer and Professor of Social and Political Theory at Oxford University, notes, who is desired and who is not is rarely random. It's a composite map that lines up neatly onto the other forms of domination and exclusion on which it lies.[7] It is in conversation with other widely held and historically entrenched beliefs about who has currency and who has power.

The idea that all human beings have equal moral worth was first advanced by European Enlightenment philosophers, particularly Immanuel Kant. Yet he also denied that non-Europeans had the same status as Europeans. He suggested there were essential intrinsic differences, particularly between white Europeans, Native Americans and Africans.[8] 'The inhabitant of the temperate[9] parts of the world, above all the central part, *has a more beautiful body* [my emphasis], works harder, is more jocular, more controlled in his passion, more intelligent than any other race of people in the world,' Kant wrote in 1761.[10]

The influential Scottish philosopher David Hume also believed black Africans were inferior to European people. In his famous footnote in the essay 'Of National Characters', Hume declared that 'I am apt to suspect the negroes, and in general all the other species of men (for there are four or five different kinds), to be naturally inferior to whites.'[11] These philosophers had cultural influence over the imagination and 'factual' beliefs of succeeding generations.[12]

Around the same time, the plantation owner and pro-slavery advocate Edward Long wrote a three-volume 'history' of Jamaica. In it, he argued that black people were not only inferior, but a different species altogether, claiming, 'An orangutan husband would not disgrace a negro woman.' Black women's hair was also described as 'a covering of wool, like the bestial fleece.'[13] Animalistic allusions became a common way to describe Africans and began to take hold in the public imagination, used to justify the brutal conditions of enslavement and later colonial expansion.[14] Black women's bodies were also coded as having an 'animal-like sexual appetite', in order to justify the systematic rape of female slaves, and later sexual harassment of domestic workers.[15] Black women were always viewed as sexually 'available' but not valuable.

When I was backpacking through South America, an acquaintance told us a 'funny' story he'd heard from his brother. At his older brother's uni, one of his flatmates, or someone he knew, anyway, lived with a white guy who would continuously fuck black women at night. As the day broke, he would make them climb out of his bedroom window, so no one would see them. Well, there's nothing that is secret that will not be known and come to light. I can only presume one of those women woke up and refused his request. I have visions of her executing an elaborate revenge, an intricately planned vengeance involving embarrassing posters, red paint over everything and a political career that this douchebag had nursed since childhood thwarted by her scathing blog. These are fantasies. I don't know what became of any of these women. All I know is that even at the time, in 2010, in the twilight of lad culture, before I'd read any bell hooks or had penetrative sex or gone on a date, I knew this was fucking despicable. I did not find the story funny at all. I held my discomfort and disgust quietly.

In her essay collection *Sista Sister*, author and influencer Candice Brathwaite talks candidly about how this value system impacted her and the way she has been treated by men. After being rejected by black boys in her teens, she dated a series of white guys through her twenties. She describes two specific examples of particularly poor treatment. One man wouldn't hold hands in public and would only introduce her as a 'dear friend'. In front of her, one of his friends tells him he clearly has 'a thing' for black women but only as trophies, never 'a wife'. Another would rarely invite her to meet his friends, never introduced her to his family and would never use the word girlfriend to describe her even after dating for a protracted amount of time. When she challenged him, he told her that he didn't see a future for them because, I kid you not, she 'saw the world in colour' and he saw it 'in black and white'.[16] It would be more accurate to say: I fancy black women but I don't value them.

Professor of Sociology Patricia Hill Collins outlines how this beauty hierarchy presents itself in the US. In her book, *Black Feminist Thought*, she writes that 'Blue-eyed, blonde, thin White women could not be considered beautiful without the Other – Black women with African features of dark skin, broad noses, full lips, and kinky hair.' 'Part of the objectification of all women lies in evaluating how they look. African-American women experience the pain of never being able to live up to the prevailing standards of beauty – standards used by White men, White women, Black men, and, most painfully, one another.'[17]

What is often accepted as natural and universal, as just what beauty *is*, is socially constructed. It's often propped up and perpetuated by media, film, television and advertising.[18] It's impossible to avoid and its ubiquity gives it the power to penetrate even the most robust defences – the armour of positive cultural reinforcement from family and specialised media that reflects your image back to you (like black beauty magazines and black beauty influencers).

'Because I've got quite a big family, naturally, I was around black people a lot of the time, but I lived in quite a heavily white area. I went to secondary school in the same sort of area,' a black male friend told me. 'That's the majority of beauty standards I saw in terms of girls who I went to school with.'

Another black male friend's family asked him outright about what they perceived to be his preference for white women. 'It's not that I don't find [black women] attractive,' he said. '[But] as a young adult, all you ever hear and all you ever see is "white women are beautiful", "that girl's so fit" – but she's white, subconsciously, I don't care how impenetrable you think you are, you will definitely receive that information and you will start to enact it. With friends it was only ever white girls that they would pick out to be attractive.'

Data shows that black people, and black men more specifically, are more likely to date someone of a different ethnic background than any other group.[19] There's nothing wrong with dating someone from a different background to you. It's good news that the acceptance of interracial relationships has increased since the 1980s. In 2020, 70 per cent of people surveyed strongly agreed with the statement: I would be happy for my child to marry someone from another ethnic group. This is a big increase in support since the last survey in 2008, where 41 per cent strongly agreed that they would happy if their child entered an interracial marriage.[20] Consenting adults should be free to love whomever they please. But it's also not inherently progressive for a black person to date a white person. It depends on the context both people come from and attitudes that frame their decisions.

I certainly wasn't immune to the 'preference' dynamics that affected my black male friends. I imbibed the implicit value system of my environment. I remember looking at the glossy prospectus for my secondary school, spotting a black guy in a basketball jersey (ostensibly included in a bid to display the school's diversity), and thinking oh good, at least one hottie in my year. Unfortunately, he'd actually moved back to America. By the end of my school days something had shifted – it was all Zac Efron and David Gandy. I wasn't even that into Usher any more. Context was everything. There were the exclusionary messages that came from advertising and magazines, the positive cultural reinforcement from home, and the microclimate of school, university and nightclubs.

At Manchester Uni, once I got over the initial thrill of having sex, weekday clubbing and flat parties without parental supervision, the desirability patterns I'd spotted in my teens returned. I was a sex-positive bad bitch who was desirable, depending on where I was and who was there. In some places I was premium stock and I felt invincible. Male attention was an investment in my volatile, fluctuating self-esteem. I felt beautiful and that made me feel powerful. Although a woman must be humble and it is a crime to be conceited, so you had to pretend you were aloof and unbothered at all times. You had to frame things the way men did, as sexual conquests, which was acceptable because sex is fun. Sometimes, it wasn't about sex, not really, it was about being desired by someone other people also thought was attractive.

In other contexts, my value depreciated rapidly until I disappeared completely; invisible, a negative number.

Male attention x social setting scale (1 = highest)

1. Hip-hop and R&B club night
2. Dancehall club night
3. Grime night in gentrified neighbourhood
4. Reggae/dub club night
5. Hipster house party
6. House/techno club night
7. Eccentric posh people house party
8. Athletics Union (AU) social
9. Debate society
10. Friday night Bop
50. Indie club night

I knew desire to be malleable and not simply about innate 'preferences' or that I just 'liked what I liked'. Only being perceived as attractive in certain contexts exposed it for the temperamental, mostly constructed, unreliable source of self-worth that it is. It's empty calories. It tastes great in the short-term and brings temporary joy, but it has no nutritional value. That hasn't stopped me craving to be acknowledged as pretty and having occasional meltdowns when it's not forthcoming. A friend once told me that she cried sometimes if she was out in a club and no one hit on her. I know I have cried too.

This isn't because I feel entitled to desire. I'm way too proud to beg to be fancied. It's because beauty is bigger than individual self-esteem. It's also a resource that's more available to some people and harder for others to access. Not only have women been socialised to seek value through being desirable, it can also be a logical response, a way to gain some power, to feel good when liberation is elusive.

'Feminine beauty and physical attractiveness are forms of capital,' writes the sociologist Meeta Rani Jha in her book *The Global Beauty Industry*. 'Physical attractiveness, whiteness, and youthfulness have accrued capital just as darker skin color, hair texture, disability, and aging have devalued feminine currency.'[21] There are material benefits to being seen as pretty: better career opportunities and pay, better treatment, a partner with higher economic, social and cultural capital.[22] Its value is based on how we are perceived by others and not how we see and define ourselves. Even though I know I'm a bad bitch, that may not necessarily change the way others see me or the power I have.

One weekend, my friend Dora took three of us to a house party in the upper reaches of North London. It was 2015 and we were twenty-four years old and relatively new to the city. We lived in flats about an hour from the party in various directions. One woman was my ex-friend, let's call her Sonia. The other was Michelle from school who was muddling through a post-breakup fog, looking for some brief artificial light while she waited for clearer skies. She'd sent a desperate text about needing to do something, go somewhere, anywhere.

Our ex-friend Sonia was by the bathroom talking to Dora about how many women were jealous of her because she was so hot. Since school, she'd had trouble bonding with women, the jealousy and not her personality or behaviour the solvent that made these friendships dissolve. Dora caught my eye across the hallway and with only a fleeting moment of eye contact sent the message: 'Is this bitch serious?!'

The only eligible bachelor was a nondescript white guy with brown hair and a humanities degree. Dora and I were on the dancefloor, where the smoke machine and UV lights kept us entertained and away from trouble. Meanwhile, Sonia and my friend from home began a head-to-head battle for supremacy, the two blondes fighting it out for the attention of this kind of characterless white male. It was *Love Island*, live. Who would win and who would be mugged off?

It became obvious that Sonia had nothing in common with this man. Michelle, however, bonded with him over a mutual appreciation of Geography. So 'friend from home' won and got the coveted phone number. They were never going to meet up, but that was never the point. Sonia was livid.

The next morning, sitting on the steps outside our shared house, Sonia was ranting about Michelle.

'How could she do that when I was talking to him first?' she asked.

'I mean . . . I think they just had more in common,' I replied. 'And you know, you did the same thing to me in a club, like, two weeks ago.'

She burst into tears because I 'wasn't being supportive' and stormed upstairs to her room. I couldn't pretend to be sad for her. I found it impossible to be. She wasn't sad about the agony of rejection and refusal at an age when you're desperate for recognition. It was anger born of entitlement. I couldn't fathom having so much entitlement to desire, that everyone should want me at all times. We were living in different realities.

Whatever game we were all playing was clearly a game for fools. It was a rigged game with a hierarchy that, as it stood, I could never reach the top of. I was never under any illusion that I was universal in my appeal. But it was also obvious this shit wasn't really working for anyone. Even our 'wins' were compromised. I started to sense a freedom in knowing that, although I didn't feel it all the time.

We're all in the crosshairs of messages telling us what we should look like and aspire to in our day-to-day lives. From 2019–2021, Parliament's Women and Equalities Select Committee carried out an inquiry into body image. They asked for contributions from experts and ran a survey into body image between 6 and 19 July 2020, which received 7,878 responses. The findings were unsurprising but no less dispiriting for that. From teenagers to women in their late fifties, exposure to media depicting unrealistic and narrowly defined beauty ideals was causing body dissatisfaction in those who did not meet them. It was especially acute for disabled women, fat women, women of colour and trans people. Sixty-nine per cent of the ethnic minorities who responded to the survey said they were more likely to 'never' or 'rarely' see themselves reflected in images in media and advertising compared with 56 per cent of white respondents.

This may come as a surprise to the very angry (white) Twitter users I've scrolled past, lamenting that 'every advert has a black person in it these days'. But when it comes to beauty campaigns by big corporates, the academic Margaret Hunter notes that this is normally an 'illusion of inclusion' that often deploys a light-skinned women of colour with Eurocentric features in some of their advertisements to build a myth that our skin colour and body types are being validated more than they actually are. A proximity to whiteness increases the chance of being featured.[23]

The Women and Equalities Committee also found that although people were curating their social media feeds by following people who looked like them, on the whole adults and young people said they felt pressured to make changes to their bodies and their appearance anyway. One of the most persistent causes of body dissatisfaction reported by women of colour was colourism.[24]

• • •

In 2017, I took part in a Radio 1 and 1Xtra documentary, *Too Dark to Mention*, about how colourism affects young people in the UK.[25] Colourism is prejudice or discrimination against people with a dark skin tone that is typically, but not always, perpetuated by people of the same ethnic group. It's often, although again not always, a colonial hangover, where beauty is measured in its inches from whiteness.* As I was ransacking my memories for examples, I found one. I remembered sitting in the hairdresser in my early teens, reading a black hair magazine with my older cousin as I waited to get my hair relaxed (straightened with toxic chemicals). There had been a beauty contest and in this issue the winners and runners-up had been announced.

'Who do you think is the prettiest?' she asked me.

'This one. She should have won,' I said, pointing at the runner-up, a lighter-skinned, black and white, mixed-heritage girl, with loose curls. A dark-skinned black girl had won.

'Nah that's bad. You just think that because she's mixed-race.'

'No, that's not why!'

It was why. She was right.

I'd started relaxing my hair when I was about twelve. I had a lot of hair and it was considered 'good' because it has a looser curl pattern. It never occurred to me to question why I so desperately wanted my hair to be straight in the first place. Until I was thirteen and trying to get out of my school's swimming lessons. After falling off a float at a birthday party and nearly drowning, I was scared of the water and had stopped my classes. Out of embarrassment for my lack of swimming skills, I would do anything to get out of it, lest I be laughed at for being rubbish. So I set about looking for evidence online that relaxed hair shouldn't be in contact with chlorine, which took me into some black haircare forums. Among tips for stretching out your

* For example, in India it predates British imperialism but in Jamaica and the US is a legacy of enslavement.

regrowth and preventing 'frizz', a post read something like: 'We need to stop doing this as black women and love ourselves. Why are we so desperate to look like white people??'

My tacit belief that I was more beautiful with straight hair, and my suspicion that this woman was onto something, would play on my mind for another thirteen years in an eddy of cognitive dissonance and denialism. This wasn't playing with different hair-styles which lots of us enjoy – I kept my hair straight on my five-month gap year backpacking around South America, when it would have been much simpler to put it in braids. I got a very expensive Brazilian blow-dry instead. By the end of the trip I had five months' regrowth to contend with. I thought straight hair or loose curls that fall wistfully as a light breeze ruffles them, or as sociologist, writer and broadcaster Emma Dabiri calls it, 'a sleek facsimile of whiteness',[26] made me look better. That message was coming from somewhere, somewhere indefinable, but certainly external, place.

'My best friend was white, and she was tall and blonde and had blue eyes and I remember wanting to be her so badly. I wanted thin lips!! Because that was what I thought was beautiful. I've got big, thick lips. Now, they're in fashion thanks to the [Kardashian] Wests,' the comedian London Hughes told Jane Garvey and Fi Glover on their *Fortunately* podcast. She told them that she used to pray at night to wake up white and blonde. 'Currently, right now, I've got someone else's hair on my head. This is Malaysian hair. My hair's an afro. I've got a massive afro. It's, like, past my elbows. But instead of wearing my afro, I wear European hair to fit in and be, like, hey I'm just like you white women. I've done it pretty much all my life.'[27]

This isn't true for all black women. As much as the beauty norms born of white supremacy shaped my desire to relax my hair, I never wanted to be white and blonde. Once in primary school, a girl asked me if I'd ever wanted to be white and I answered with a definitive no. As someone who went natural in my late twenties, I have few styling skills and my attempt at absorbing them through YouTube tutorials have resulted in little but lack-lustre twist outs. I was not one of the many black women who, finding all the salons and hair shops closed, used the Covid-19 pandemic to teach themselves how to braid.[28] I emerged from the lockdown with dry coils covered in the chalky-white film of Cantu leave-in conditioner. My hair was also significantly shorter on one side of my head than the other for reasons unknown. I'm still looking for the right hair products that work for me, yet to find the glass slipper that fits perfectly. Although I'm enjoying being able to do swimming lessons without stress and no longer running for cover from the rain.

In winter, I tend to put my hair in braids to protect it from the elements but also because I'm lazy. I can't be arsed with the time-consuming co-washes and treatments that don't easily slot into a morning routine that can be derailed by a manager putting in a last-minute meeting for 9 a.m. Some black women use wigs in the same way, as a time-saving protective styling. My female cousins often switch it up between wigs, braids and straight hair because, why not? Experimenting with styles can be a way to express yourself. It's not always that deep.

I keep my hair in afro-textured styles as a personal statement of rejection of the messages that were so powerful and pervasive I believed them to be my own thoughts. I stopped relaxing my hair in 2016, after a (black) friend had essentially asked me: 'What would Malcolm say?' We had both recently finished Dora's copy of the *Autobiography of Malcolm X*, where he slams his former self for straightening his hair with chemicals. I had no defence that felt genuine and, not one to admit defeat, I just stopped relaxing it. It was the beginning of a journey of divest-ment and self-acceptance and my hair reminds me of that, even when it's dry.

This was the same year I started writing about dating for *gal-dem*. Over the years, the power structures that shape my life, our world, so fundamentally that they seem our own invention, had increasingly revealed themselves, even in the most intimate parts of my life. Feeling like a celebrity at Notting Hill Carnival and and this weird hippy party in Bristol, where a nearly all-white crowd attended a celebration of black music at the Malcom X Centre, and a ghostlike nobody at indie nights in Manchester. The ex-boyfriend from university who sent me the odd treatise on race from the white male's perspective while 'finding himself' in India. The devil's advocate who asked whether 'Cecil Rhodes was really that bad' after sex. The racist Republican. The reason I'd been attracted to any of these guys in the first place. Why was I so craven for approval and praise from all men, but especially white men? It was all connected. The separate tentacles of these experiences were joined at the head of white male heteropatriarchy. For better or worse, I worked through all those realisations online, where they live on in the ether that is the internet, a living document of past insecurities and political awakenings.

Around this time, I took part in my first ever panel discussion called *Love, Sex and Desire in a White World*. A member of the audience shared a story about her uncle, who would consistently date white women because he felt they were 'a prize', the ultimate trophy. She was embarrassed, frustrated but also offended and pained: could he not see what he was implicitly saying about her and her value? That same year, the YouTube comedy channel VanBanter made a viral video. In it, mostly dark-skinned black men around Stratford, East London, were asked by the host what their 'type' was. The video was a reel of insults towards dark-skinned women and a veneration of lighter-skinned, mixed-race women. Phrases like 'light-skins with 3B curly hair and a big back only', 'no dark skins' and 'no black girls like my shoes' were common.[29] Naturally, the video was dragged online for its display of internalised racism, misogynoir and self-hate.

But all these conversations about race and desirability felt confined to a subset of spaces: between people of colour on- and offline, a *Vice* article here and there and a Channel 4 documentary that briefly set Twitter alight.

Then along came *Love Island.*

• • •

Figuring out my life, albeit in public, had started to pay dividends. I took a break from dating white men, to figure out who I was when not thrown against a sharp white background. My teenage self had been right all along, even if it didn't feel that way at the time – focus on your friends and your studies. Everything else is a bonus. I'd subbed studies for work and found a day job that I believed in, doing research and campaigning on race and inequality and letting the work consume me. This consummation wasn't always healthy. But I had something to care about that was bigger than the minutiae of my life and it enabled me to divest more easily from what men thought of me, reduced the constant need to be validated by them, and made me more able to cope with rejection. I was still very much a messy bitch with anxiety who lived for the drama. But I was tired of so much of my personal life being a spectacle and a political question, so I turned the lens outward.

Unfortunately, I then got sucked into *Love Island* and I felt twenty-two all over again.

I started watching *Love Island* in 2018, three years after ITV rebooted the show. When I was travelling, I'd given up sugar and many a staple TV show out of necessity – there often wasn't any sugar in the hostels and you can't watch the nightly soaps when you're backpacking. So I didn't bother with shows like *Love Island* that are on most weeknights and require an overwhelming commitment. In the summer of 2018, however, I was between flats and staying with various friends who would have it on in the background. It wasn't long before I was hooked.

Thanks to the *Love Island*-opinion-piece industrial complex, at least once a year we get to have a conversation about race and dating, inspired by the sealed fates of dark-skinned black contestants. Like the show itself, each iteration tends to follow the same script. The conversation is so tired that some writers just link to the article they wrote about it two years prior, rather than trying to reinvent the wheel.

Over seven series, the kick-off 'coupling' session in episode one has seen a black contestant picked last. While black/white mixed-heritage contestants generally tend to do well (especially the men), dark-skinned black people do not. An overwhelming number of male contestants cite their 'type' as a (white) woman with blonde hair and blue eyes so pervasively black Twitter is awash with jokes about eugenics. The first year I tuned into the show was also the first year there was a black female contestant who wasn't light-skinned, Samira Mighty. It was not fun viewing. After repeated rejections, she breaks down in tears to fellow contestants Megan and Dani. The guy she likes – Frankie – fancies Megan, who has dyed blonde hair. Through tears Samira says to Megan: 'I'm just me and you're you.'

The trend continued the next year with black Twitter fan favourite Yewande Bilal. Speaking to *Cosmopolitan* magazine, she said she had: 'personally struggled a lot because every man who came into the villa said their type was "blonde hair and blue eyes". I just sat there like, "Obviously I missed the memo because I'm not blonde and I definitely won't have blue eyes." It was a struggle and I cried so much.'[30]

Putting someone into an environment where they are separated from all their family and friends, under the relentless gaze of cameras and social media, requires care (something the show only seemed to factor in after three tragic deaths by suicide by former contestants). Is it really that hard to cast some contestants who fancy black people so it's not such a car crash year in, year out? I no longer judged the contestants as I had with the woman on *Dating in the Dark*. I blamed the producers of the show. Yet I kept watching.

I love reality TV, but I watch it primarily as entertainment. I don't expect it to be realistic. *Love Island* is almost too realistic. Like dating apps, it takes everything that's terrible about dating culture and beauty standards and magnifies it, enlarging it until the detail is distorted and nuance is erased, leaving us with something lurid and garish. In a piece on the almost pathological obsession with women with blonde hair and blue eyes in series seven, journalist Diyora Shadijanova wrote that watching the show as a woman of colour takes its toll. 'I've spent years uncoupling from exclusive beauty standards and trying my best to decentre men's opinions on my body,' she said. 'However, watching these hugely loaded dynamics play out on *Love Island* time and time again – regardless of how much I try to resist the narratives in my head – feels like taking a million steps backward in self-love and self-acceptance.'[31] I agree. But even when the show triggered suppressed insecurities that sent me spiralling into vivid re-enactments of past rejections and invisibility, I stopped watching the show only at the beginning of series seven.

I started to go off the show in series six, the first winter addition of *Love Island*. A black contestant, Mike Boateng, paired up with Leanne, who is also black. When he told fellow islander, Jess Gale, a white, blonde woman with lip fillers, that he was leaning towards Leanne over her, she told him she was 'shocked at this strong preference'. Although her twin sister Eve Gale says she doesn't think this reaction had anything to do with race, I'm unconvinced. It came across that Jess couldn't believe Mike was more attracted to Leanne than her because she's white and blonde and Leanne is black.

The flurry of *Love Island*-racism think pieces that proliferated in 2021 captured my mood. We can just . . . stop watching the show, they argued. On Metro.co.uk Nike, the co-founder of Stop Erasing Black Women, said she'd switched to *Love Island* US, a show that, although not free of desirability politics or colourism, at least had dark-skinned black women in the cast being desired.[32]

The writer Ebony Purks told *Insider* readers to turn off *Love Island* UK and tune into the second season of the Netflix show *Too Hot to Handle* instead, where multiple black female contestants were desired and pursued by men of different ethnicities.[33]

After the first episode of the 2022 summer *Love Island*, founder and CEO of the online magazine *Black Ballad*, Tobi Oredein, wrote that she would no longer be watching the show. Although *Love Island* producers had changed the format of the opening episode to avoid black women being picked last, she decided she would rather follow the show from a distance. 'Sometimes I want to learn when watching television, but ultimately I want escapism and the truth is *Love Island* doesn't offer that. Yes, there are laughs but the laughs are so overshadowed by how the men in the show see the beauty of black women,' she said.[34]

I stopped watching the season before Tobi, after a conversation between some of the contestants that compared 'discriminating' against cis-women who've had plastic surgery to racism simply ended me.

The show sets up inane challenges for contestants as episode filler. This episode had the Mr and Mrs competition, where coupled-up pairs have to answer questions about each other. This time, instead of asking them to speculate about their favourite sex position or how many people they've slept with, the men were asked to guess which cosmetic surgeries their female partners had. The women were not asked about the men – revealing less about the contestants and more about the producers who cast them. Only one woman, Kaz Kamwi, had not gone under the knife or had any injections. The rest had at least had lip fillers, if not Botox and a boob job too.

Later in the challenge, one of the male contestants, Hugo Hammond, was asked what his biggest turn-off was and told the group he wasn't a fan of 'fake personality and looks'. He repeated the word 'fake' a bizarre number of times, which incited an equally bonkers response from fellow contestants Faye Winter and Sharon

Gaffka. Faye instructed Hugo 'to get fucking educated' as if cosmetic surgery were a justice issue and not just a consumer choice – a decision incubated by sexist social pressures but an individual choice nonetheless. Sharon tops it off by comparing his comments to someone saying they 'wouldn't date you because of your race'. Nearly every guy to that point had said their type was 'blonde hair and blue eyes' and Kaz (who is black) had not demanded crying apologies from the men because they were effectively excluding her. The show is at its most interesting, but also most tiresome, when it reveals who expects to be desired most of the time and who is presumed to be excluded as par for the course. I muted #LoveIsland on Twitter for three months and felt at peace.

I have a lot of compassion for the desire for cosmetic surgery. I wanted it desperately throughout my teenage years. I ordered a costly, dodgy herbal tablet that was certainly a placebo that promised to make my boobs grow. That pressure is still felt by young people. In the government's inquiry into body image, 31 per cent of under-eighteens had considered cosmetic surgery and 35 per cent had considered non-surgical treatments like Botox and fillers. The academic Hua Wen calls the decision to have cosmetic surgery an individual solution to the inequalities of sexism, ageing, and classism, although at great cost and high risk.[35] And as Professor Heather Widdows notes in her book *Perfect Me*,[36] when beauty is valued so highly and comes with rewards, it is a rational choice for women to pursue it and enjoy the benefits. But just because something feels good doesn't mean it's inherently a good thing.

The stuff we do in the name of beauty needs to be framed as what it actually is – complicit freedom. Or, as I saw someone write on Twitter in reference to her own non-invasive surgery: lip fillers aren't praxis. Beauty is contradictory. It can be an act of resistance and refusal – like growing my relaxer out, feeling pretty in environments where it's not being affirmed and having no desire to use skin lighteners. But it often isn't. Sometimes you're just getting your nails done. Beauty can empower and disempower, be fun and pleasurable and exclusionary and unequal. But maybe it could be better, something less important and valued.

• • •

'We're all capable of making choice(s) and doing what we want, but what happens when what we want matches up with a kind of complicity around what is valued?' author and academic Claudia Rankine asked a *Vogue* interviewer. She was discussing her book *Just Us: An American Conversation*, where she explores blondeness and how it connects to ideas about whiteness.[37] It made me consider choices I make in the name of beauty that fit this mould: when I used to relax my hair, my braids, getting my eyebrows done. Feminism has freed me from the practices that felt the most constraining. I rarely wear heels, which I used to wear daily as a teen. I stopped shaving and waxing, no longer ripping my hair out of damp crevices around my body and paying £50 for the privilege. Although being hairy is not a beauty norm for women, it is much more popular now than when I was in school, so it's a choice that other people have made easier for me. I make all these decisions freely but they are heavily influenced by the prevailing fashions of femininity.

Towards the end of her book on beauty and women's lives, the journalist Autumn Whitefield-Madrano concluded that when we talk about beauty we anchor it in the personal. It's all 'body image workbooks and workshops, personal essays in women's magazines about triumphing over self-loathing,' she said. 'All give the individual a much-needed boost, but for the most part that's where it ends.'[38]

In the government's inquiry into beauty standards, one of the recommendations is better regulation. People felt bombarded by images and advertising on social media and more broadly that made them feel lacking, that encouraged them to change themselves. They wanted images that had been Photoshopped labelled as such and for influencers to own up to the cosmetic surgery they've had. Beauty still matters, especially for women. So the more people who could be included in that the better. I have appreciated and benefitted from these attempts at inclusion by brands and fashion magazines. It also makes me more likely to buy their products, which I'm sure is the point.

'I wonder what it would be like to grow up in a world where being beautiful is not seen as a necessity, but instead a nice thing some people are born with and some people aren't, like a talent for swimming, or playing the piano,' the journalist and author Megan Nolan wrote in the *New York Times*. 'What if we stopped prioritizing pleasing aesthetics above so much else?'[39]

I want to live in a society where beauty is viewed as something more contextual, with value judgements not made in an entirely superficial way.* And while I know having more black models in advertising and in *Vogue* isn't freedom, I still love to see it. Don't listen to the Instagram therapists who instruct women to say, 'Your joy brings me happiness' to friends, rather than 'I love your skirt' or 'You look amazing.' I want to be complimented on my appearance, although not by strangers in the street who expect something in return for their commentary. I enjoy light-touch makeup rituals, getting my hair done and styling an outfit that says exactly what I'm feeling. I just don't place all my worth on it.

* For more on this as a way of seeing, read Dabiri, E. (Penguin 2019) *Don't Touch My Hair*, p.173.

7 Awkward sexual awakening: the queen of casual sex

Due to a bizarre obsession with the *High School Musical* franchise in 2007, the girls got me a Zac Efron calendar for my sixteenth birthday. You weren't able to stalk celebrities online back then the way you can now. I'm grateful that famous people didn't have social media accounts in 2007, as I would have 1,000 per cent stalked the cast, turning up to their hotels and building bonds with other die-hard fans in the foyer. Fortunately for my internet history, a calendar was as good as it got. In many of the images he was shirtless, the closest I'd ever been to a six-pack. So naturally, when I saw one in the flesh I lost my fucking mind and did not know how to behave.

For one year of uni, I was the queen of casual sex (or at least in the narrative thread I'd cross-stitched into elaborate patterns in my head). From the University of Manchester to the University of Toronto, I reigned. In reality, I'd had sex with four or so people (depending on what you count as sex), a 300 per cent increase on the previous year. Exponential growth. I was finally the main character.

During my teens, I didn't have any of those formative faux-romantic relationships, where you hold hands and get dumped in the space of a week. I didn't kiss anyone until I was sixteen and my sexual experiences were infrequent and limited. University changed that and having had sex multiple times now meant I was no longer worrying if boys liked me. I wish I could say that my path to self-acceptance began in the library surrounded by feminist texts but, sadly, the starting pistol was casual sex. The dull headache of anxiety lifted. I was desirable after all. No longer being preoccupied by that freed up a lot of space for thoughts about other things.

I started filling in the newly available headspace with a newly popular concept called 'feminism', no longer the preserve of women who didn't know how to have fun and hated makeup. As shallow as my feminism was at the time, at least the puddle was there. I could syphon off just enough to nourish the ground and make it fertile enough for new ideas to take root and sprout. I used the remaining pockets of mental capacity, the crevices between postcolonial theories and worrying if the gaps in my eyebrows would ever grow back after overplucking them in the early 2000s, to make a list of the guys I wanted to hook up with before I left for an exchange semester at the University of Toronto.

I completed the list, triumphantly ticking them off one by one in my head like a perverse to-do list, the sweet release of serotonin from all that external validation more pleasurable than the sex itself. There was a lot to figure out about love and sex and power and my knowledge was limited. I had the Spark Notes of feminism and patriarchy, a cheat sheet of top lines but without any serious analysis or deep understanding. I thought being a modern woman was to mimic the most basic and clichéd masculinity, a belief I'd picked up from popular culture. This was the era of TV shows that if aired now, would be eviscerated on social media and the topic of infinite think pieces. This was the time of *Entourage*, *Girls Gone Wild* and *Girl Power*. Women could drink guys under the table and be rowdy too. You could have sex with as many people as you liked and no one could do anything about it.

The smoking area

Is there anything more sensual than a smoking area? Created in response to the 2007 public smoking ban, they became incubators of sexual tension, the air always heavy with poisonous vapours and possibility. Your hair is frowsy with stale smoke but your outfit and attitude are fresh and you know it. Finally, some respite from the sweat and heat and chaos of the club. Anyone in possession of a lighter or a spare cigarette becomes a target for a temporary friendship. Alongside the women's toilet, the smoking area is top-tier and I cherish the conversations had there with people I'll probably never see again.

It's October 2011 and I'm out for a Dancehall night in a club on the edge of Manchester's Northern Quarter, a building that started life as a Victorian mill and has now inevitably matured into an upmarket restaurant. It was the final stand in the smoking area, the waiting room before the Magic-Bus-to-Pizza-Champion journey home. Unfortunately, I had a tic at uni where if I fancied someone I was unable to look at them directly, my eyes darting up and down in a frenzy of avoidance. So when I spot someone hot on the periphery of the group, I intuitively force my focus onto an imaginary optician's chart in the distance: across, diagonal, down, across.

Then this guy held my arm for a reason I can no longer remember and stared directly into my eyes and held my gaze. His arms wore the curves and bends of effortful gym sessions.

'Who was that? In the smoking area?'

'Oh, that's [redacted].'

Inexplicably, I knew one day we would have sex.

I remember the first semester of my second year at uni in terms of significant parties. The events act as units of time: getting a photo with a towel-clad Ghostface Killah of Wu Tang Clan fame, the four trips to the Warehouse Project, a well-known Manchester club series that runs through the winter months, the two house parties we threw and the festivals that closed the summer of 2012. I've blocked out the passive aggressive Facebook posts about the cleaning rota, mugs that doubled up as ashtrays and the mould that had colonised my pink pan in the second kitchen (for which no one took responsibility). I loved parties because I love meeting new people and I love to dance badly in public places, but also because I love stories, and parties, like conflict, drive narratives. People confess to things, they behave selfishly and they hook up. Sometimes, you can dine out on the drama from one party for weeks. They are the signposts that direct the plot onwards. Even through the fog of booze and narcotics and the decade that's passed, the memories of the parties stand out.

The house party

A few weeks after the sexually charged smoking area, my housemates and I decided to throw a big party. We lived on a road of large, red-brick terraced houses in the centre of the student area. If a house on our road had a party, it was customary that anyone who happened to be walking past it was allowed to drop in. It was bad form to have a strict door policy, like not bringing a bottle of wine to a dinner party or asking someone you just met if they're 'seeing anyone special at the moment'.

Our house was dilapidated, which made it perfect for debauchery. The downstairs kitchen that had never seen a refurb, mice scurrying in the walls and a toilet simply called 'the mushroom one' because it had live fungi growing in the corner. You didn't have to worry about causing damage as everything was already broken. You set up speakers and DJ equipment on the counters, turn the main lights down and your rented strobe lights on.

We had a patchwork of about a hundred miscellaneous people: poshos in striped or checked shirts, our friends who'd come up from our various hometowns, guys who had legitimately made it out of ends and the guys cosplaying as poor. Wisps of weed and cigarette smoke sat suspended over the mattress as guests sat and exhaled. I did my first line of cocaine with some randoms in the bathroom.

I stumbled out of the bathroom and into [redacted].

'I've just done cocaine for the first time.'

'Oh shit. Did you really need that?'

'Probably not. No. But I've never done it before and it was free.'

I am suddenly overcome with confidence as the cocaine kicks in. I am the baddest bitch that ever lived.

'Do you want to stay?' I say, maybe. (Let's be honest. I don't remember. I was high.)

Halloween at Factory

A week later, it was time for Halloween. I've now seen a six-pack in real life so I have an unwavering conviction in my sauce. The year before, misguided by the film *Mean Girls*, my flatmate and I had dressed up as sexy animals (I a bunny and she a cat) only to find the rules had changed and now dressing as a truly horrifying beast was in vogue. Perhaps your outfit was tight but your face was to be unrecognisable, violent with fake blood and cheap too-thick creamy-white paint. I learnt my lesson and so this time, I actually dressed up as something Halloween-related. I went with a classic of the genre, a basic attempt at a Día de los Muertos skull on my face courtesy of my flatmate Lorna.

'You're not going to be able to pull with that,' my flatmate told me.

'Watch me.'

I managed to pull a guy from one of my History modules, who if memory serves me, I gave the most lacklustre blow job of all time. But no matter – he had been on the list and I could tick him off. I wasn't trying to build a reputation based on prowess or even competency. I just wanted to be desired, because being desired was a kind of power, currency even, and finally I felt like I was in credit instead of debt.

I hate to admit it, but knowing multiple men were attracted to me gave me more confidence and security than any of the formative texts I read during that time. A tinnitus of anxiety that buzzed lightly in my head was muted. 'Beauty is not good capital,' academic Tressie McMillan Cottom writes in her essay collection, *Thick*. 'It compounds the oppression of gender. It is not useful for human flourishing. Beauty is, like all capital, merely valuable.'[1]

And it was valuable for a time. Sex is pretty fun, as is attention. But sex often involves other people and other people are chaotic and you can't control how their behaviour will affect you. I knew this was a temporary phase of my life – unpredictable, shallow, pleasurable and entertaining. I was cashing out while my stock was up. I'd already learnt other ways to build worth, namely cultural capital and likability. These have their limits too, but definitely have a longer shelf life than being desirable.

Roadhouse revisited

Months later, I'm back at the old Victorian mill, song after song taking me back to my childhood, a soundtrack of songs no one at school knew except the girl with a second home in the Caribbean and a black boyfriend. I'd spotted [redacted] in the crowd, and he was acting strangely. Men were like that, so it wasn't much of a concern (I'd read *The Game* by journalist turned pick-up artist Neil Strauss). When I'm ready to leave, I decide to pick up one of the black cabs from outside the club (a luxury I could occasionally afford in Manchester, shout out to the Manchester Advantage Scholarship). I spot a pink card on the floor by my feet, the driving licence of a pretty girl who lived in south-east of England. The next day, I buy an envelope and post the ID back to the address on the licence with a note that read something like:

Found this in a cab outside Roadhouse.
Hope you had a good night!
Kimberly McIntosh x

(My full name so she could find me on Facebook.)

Her address suggested she lived in the Home Counties.

She adds me on Facebook and DMs to thank me. We have one mutual friend: [redacted].

Some random house party and the (first) end of Store Street

I'm at a random house party chatting with a friend over the banister, me on the steps and him on the ground. [Redacted] is coming down the stairs.

'Hi.'

'Hi.' It's stilted and awkward but guys are like that so I don't think much of it. After he descends the stairs my friend asks me: 'Did you get with him?'

'A few weeks ago. Why?'

'I'm pretty sure he has a girlfriend. I know someone that lives with him. Plus, apparently he has a different accent when he talks to his nan. He's actually from, like, Buckinghamshire or something.'

Shit. Although I know it wasn't my fault, I feel somehow responsible.

At the final Warehouse Project I've got booked, the last season at the Store Street venue for a while and my last before I fly off for study abroad, I think I see a flash of him and his girlfriend in the crowd. Although, it might be a mirage or just some strong MDMA.

The frat house and the co-op

'Hi Egerton Roaders! Just to say I will be sending a card to the house in the coming weeks as no one writes letters any more and I feel this should change. I have lost all my ID, money, camera and library card at a frat house so just to let you know I'm still a sensible, well-rounded person. *Te extraño** xxx' – I post in our house share Facebook group in January 2012. I've been in Canada for a matter of days.

I've just moved to Toronto, the Canadian New York. It's freezing, but everyone tells me 'It's actually a really warm winter.' Instead of using my scholarship money to buy a proper quilted coat, I hit the mall on Yonge and Dundas and buy an oversized faux-fur one in the Forever 21 sale. One of the other Brits, my now close friend Daniel, invites a group of us to a party at the co-operative housing complex he lives in. That is where I meet the American.

There's talk of a party at a frat house.

'The frat party will be lame. The frats aren't as good here,' he says. He cannot believe I've voluntarily chosen Canada over the United States when there was an option to go to numerous US colleges instead. He is only here because he got kicked out of school: he got drunk, stole a golf cart and crashed it – but don't worry – Daddy got him into one of Canada's most competitive universities!

Unfortunately, the frat party isn't all that, so a group of us head back to the co-op. I have a beer with the American who tells me he is a Republican, which I believe to be a joke as I am still high on the post-racial, change is coming, Obama hype. He's classic American white-guy attractive, he wouldn't look out of place in the cast of *Grease*, leant against a fifties convertible with a leather jacket and a cigarette. He is literally screaming 'I'M RACIST AND ALL MY FAMILY ARE RACISTS' but I'm not seeing it because I'm yet to discover racist people are still very capable of being attracted to black people.

It didn't present itself immediately, when I woke up in my faux-fur coat lying on his bathroom floor, my belongings AWOL but my cheeks soothed by the cool chill of the tiles on my bare body. It showed up five months later, at a party back at the same co-op.

---

* 'I miss you' in Spanish. I'd been taking some modules at uni.

He believed black people are predisposed to violence, which where I'm from is called biological racism (but I wasn't like that – just the other blacks!). He held his views in a way that was casual and unconsidered, in the way that people will advocate for the British version of *The Office* without having seen the American version, an unquestioned presumption based on a belief of superiority.

People's beliefs and values are drawn from the well of their experiences and the nebulous structures that shape our lives. That doesn't just stay in their heads though, it is often the driving force behind their behaviour too, the way they treat other people, and how we respond. 'We must not think that by saying yes to sex one says no to power,' Michel Foucault wrote in *The Will to Knowledge*.[2] Something I thought was light-hearted and uncomplicated had in just six months shown itself to be knotty and layered. Sex was loaded with power dynamics and having it didn't always make me feel powerful. I didn't feel empowered or in control at all.

The festivals

That summer, I finished up in Canada and headed for San Francisco. I spent a month in an RV with three friends and a group of strangers, touring the West Coast of the US. It was like being in a season of *The Real World* – RV edition. There were bust-ups and hook-ups and running around the MGM hotel and casino in Vegas with a bottle of vodka. It was seeing scenery so astounding I got a sudden urge to cry. I topped it off with a week on the lakes of Northern Ontario and a last-minute shag in the laundry room of a frat house because why the fuck not. 'Having sex can bring about other valued effects – connection, intimacy, bonding,' writes the author and academic Katherine Angel. 'We must also be careful not to rule out sex itself as capable of providing these.'[3]

There's nothing wrong with casual sex itself, the problems lie elsewhere.

I got a paid internship back home and saved for the final activities of the summer: the festivals. I went to two back-to-back in Croatia, solely partying at the first one and working the second. It is an energy only someone in their early twenties could muster. It was a glorious hedonism, and the kind of summer I'll probably never have again.

At the first festival, I was coming out of my tent when I swore I spotted [redacted] by the toilets with a girl but put it down as a second mirage conjured by the Croatian heat and the drugs.

At the second festival, I was on the wristbands and my friend was on stewarding. I stood with her one evening as she marshalled people in and out of one of the stages. I heard someone behind me call my name. It is the girl who lost her ID in the taxi outside the Victorian mill nightclub. Her boyfriend – [redacted] – is straggling behind.

'Thank you so much for posting my ID back to me,' she says. She tells me they are moving in together. I am awe-struck. He is silent.

As they depart, he whispers, 'What are the fucking chances', audible only to me.

I've had enough. I go back to uni in September and don't have sex with anyone until I get into a relationship.

8 Fear and loathing on a Hackney Downs mattress

I was sixteen when I had my first kiss and I immediately threw up all over the bed. It was April 2007 and my friend Lara texted me to ask what I was up to. I was sixteen years old and living in a commuter town, so obviously I was up to absolutely nothing at all. Lara was the kind of girl who wasn't afraid of boys, not even older ones, and nearly always had a boyfriend. She was the kind of girl that a boy in the year above would text to say they were renting a room at the Ibis hotel, a no-frills chain in the centre of town, to get pissed in. I was the kind of girl to tag along. I told Mum I was staying at Heather's house. Heather had middle-class parents with hippy tendencies who lived in a large suburban house with light boho touches. It was the kind of place you could show up to at 3 a.m. without question. We met the boys at the hotel, drank Smirnoff Ice and had a fight with the shower, taking turns to spray water at each other from its head. I kissed someone's friend, a guy who claimed he'd been kicked out of his parents' house, although on reflection, it was probably just the annex in their back garden. The Smirnoff Ice hit too hard. I was overcome by all the sugar and low alcohol content, projectile vomiting all over the bed and, as far as I recall, not making it to the shower. For months, Lara referred to my first kiss as with the 'homeless guy'.

Finally my first kiss was done, I was no longer falling behind.

I had also thrown up shortly after, while the guy in question leapt to safety.

The morning after we were sitting in the Costa Coffee in Reading train station having recovery hot chocolates with whipped cream and marshmallows on top when my friend Dom spotted us on his way into London to watch Chelsea play. One half of my hair lay bone straight and the other frizzy from the shower fight. He told us we looked 'worse for wear' then headed off on his way. The next day he posted on my Facebook wall.

8 April 2007
Dominic Sutton wrote on your timeline
Ello ello. Still cant believe i saw u – and in such weird circumstances. Chelsea won!!! Beat the Tottenham scum.

For days shame suffocated me, an overpowering sense that I had misbehaved in some way. This wasn't from being seen in a state of disrepair. And I was more than ready to kiss and be kissed. But desire was something tinged with a patina of guilt. I had exposed my true self. I had lacked control. I would feel the same way again two years later, when at Reading Festival I had a fumble in a guy's tent that I would now call sex. I didn't back then because I thought sex meant penetration. Anything sexual seesawed between shame and empowerment, rarely reaching equilibrium.

My only strong memories of sex education are learning how to put a condom on a plastic model of a penis (not the mythical banana I'd heard mentioned on the primary school rumour mill). I think there had also been a video about childbirth for girls that served more as a scare tactic against the 2000s moral panic of teenage pregnancy.* If memory serves, no one mentioned the

* For more on the overestimation of teenage pregnancy see Duffy, B. (Atlantic Books, 2019) *Why We're Wrong About Nearly Everything: A Theory of Human Misunderstanding.*

existence of LGBTQ+ people in primary or secondary school but I can't be sure. The only thing that stuck was the importance of STI check-ups and the condom lesson, which did pay dividends when the time came to put one on, and the times I didn't and took myself to the clinic. Sex was about being in control and protecting yourself: from STIs, pregnancy and assault.

Like a lot of women my age, I got much of my sex education from *Sex and the City*. This wasn't in a technical sense. I could only infer the mechanics of sex from *Cosmopolitan*, and the more explicit sex scenes in TV shows and movies (watching porn was not an option but a dirty, shameful, guilt-inducing thing). There was one TV show, *Sexcetera*, that came on late at night, where the hosts were sometimes naked but that was it. I did not talk to my mum about sex. She pretended she had waited until marriage in a bid to delay my own experimentation. Eventually, I figured out she was pregnant with me at her wedding while looking through the wedding album and realising my birthday was a good few months less than nine months later.

So I watched *Sex and the City* to get a sense of what sex was *for*. To me, the show said that sex was about power and confidence. The power to own your choices and the power of promiscuity. Sex could be part of a relationship or just for fun with someone you never saw again, by choice. It didn't have to be a shameful thing. Reruns were airing in 2007–2008 when I was in sixth form and I watched it devotedly. This was a good thing. It gave me a framework to have sex when I felt like it and the confidence to call out sexist criticism. It didn't give me the tools to make sense of when sex makes you feel anxious, used, scared or harmed. And why should it? It's just a TV show! But the dominant stories that accompanied my coming-of-age in the 2000s and 2010s was a Spice Girls fun if vapid Girl Power and ladette culture, which involved outdoing the most loutish masculine behaviour to prove how equal you were to men. This became *lean-in* confidence feminism – by being more strident at work, power posing in the mirror and asking for more money, you too could beat sexism. This also applied to sex. Be confident in the bedroom! Know your needs! Ask for what you want! Cum every time or dump him! 'The utterly reasonable claim that women should be afforded sexual freedom – be perverse and lustful and up-for-it – slid into the more dubious insistence that women *are* and *must* be so,' academic and writer Katherine Angel wrote in her book *Tomorrow Sex Will Be Good Again*.[1] You had to be confident and constantly fucking and adventurous or you'd failed.

By the time I got to university, the seesaw had shifted all its weight towards empowerment. I wanted to lose my virginity as soon as possible. They do things differently in Manchester, so the saying goes, so it sounded like the kind of place where things happened and I could become someone things happened to. Modern and empowered women had a lot of sex with whomever they wanted and boasted about it effortlessly. I wanted to be that kind of woman.

The first time I had penetrative sex I didn't use a condom. I walked around the corner to my halls and I could feel two lines of cum making their way down, framing the inside of my legs, sluggishly pooling in the centre of my pants. I took a shower and rinsed the pants in the sink. I was finally free of my virginity, no longer stalked by the shadow of embarrassment. It wasn't about the sex, although I enjoyed that too, it was what it signalled. It said, 'Finally, I'm an adult.' And every day could be like this, with the promise of whimsy and adventure.

Then I arrived at the GUM clinic and felt less fully fledged adult and more like a naughty child. I had committed the cardinal sin of sex and ignored rule one of sex ed: use protection. I tried it with the receptionist, saying the condom broke with half-hearted commitment before giving up and just writing 'morning after pill' on the form and accepting the judgement (possibly real or simply me projecting). I booked in to get long-acting reversible contraception over Christmas. When Mum caught me trying to slink out of the house for my appointment, she simply hugged me then let me go and protect myself. The nurse at the clinic assumed that, having only had one sexual partner, he must now be my boyfriend. She asked me how long we'd been together and I lied and said a few months so she wouldn't think I was a slut.

Sex ed taught the health aspects of sex well and it mostly stuck. For the emotional, I'd taken my cues from pop culture: be cool, detached, fun and light. The cool girl trope, the deluge of movies that depicted two-dimensional women who were nonchalant, never needy and blasé about commitment has been dragged to high heaven. It was eviscerated in the 2012 book and, later, the movie adaptation of *Gone Girl*. But at the time of that book/film, when I was twenty/twenty-one years old, it didn't feel like a performance. I just didn't really care all that much and the suggestion that I did felt like an affront. No lies told, if any of the men I'd hooked up with during those years had asked me out for a meal I would have said yes. But it wasn't an expectation and I wasn't emotionally destroyed that none of them fell for me instantly and wanted to be my boyfriend. This was just what sex and dating was in the twenty-first century, a short story collection you could dip in and out of rather than a grand novel with a small set of characters. I had implicitly agreed to the terms of engagement and, apart from the guy with the secret girlfriend, no one had lied to me. Even the racist Republican had shown me who he was the first time, if I'd cared to pay attention. There were no fake promises. Having casual sex felt thrilling. I was finally embodying the adult life that in my late teens, I'd design and get lost in for hours. If you have sex in the laundry room of a Canadian frat house the day before your flight back to Heathrow it's probably not going to be the opening paragraph of your grand love story. It is what it is: sex. It's fun but, best of all, it's a good story.

• • •

It turned out I wouldn't have casual sex again for two years after landing at Terminal 5, because I went back to uni and met someone. Finally, I got a real boyfriend. I'd completed the trifecta of adulthood: sex, drugs, relationship.

Young love is an old TV show that's aged poorly. You rewatch episodes and the characters' lines curdle and the laughter that at the time felt organic suddenly sounds canned. All the emotions are lurid, high-pitched and overacted. But God, it was good at the time. Young love is the *Little Britain* of love, with hindsight it's awful. But once I became accustomed to promises and intimacy, there was no going back from that. My needs weren't transparent, they were muddied now, by emotions and insecurities. My cool-girl persona desecrated, I realised I really was, just like other girls. Post-2014, when my uni relationship ended, I could no longer have sex with the same guy more than twice because, if I did it three times, it would summon the beast of attachment.

The great thing about monogamy is that sex often gets better when you have it with the same person over and over again. There's more time for the trial and error of figuring out what you like. But the expectations increased too. I started to care about what the other person thought of me and if they were happy. Sex also became about keeping men happy and secure. This wasn't anything to do with this specific relationship, and the feelings of obligation and managing egos re-emerged in my mid-to-late twenties, long after that relationship ended. If sex-positivity is an openness towards sexuality in all its forms, with an emphasis on sexual pleasure, then lots of men haven't gotten the memo. Because power pervades sex and it's the same power dynamic that crops up in the more public parts of our lives.

The solution seems obvious: say something! But communicating is fraught enough with friends when you're fully clothed, let alone naked, both physically naked and nakedly in need of safety and praise. If talking to each other clearly were easy, Sally Rooney's books wouldn't be so popular. I tried to be more confident and assertive but that's hard, particularly with men, whose masculinity might be tied up with 'performance'.

Research in 2019 by the End Violence Against Women Coalition into public attitudes about heterosexual sex found that these feelings are common. Their survey of nearly 4,000 people revealed that 57 per cent of respondents thought women were more likely to go along with sex to keep their partner happy. This went up to 63 per cent when you asked women and down to 50 per cent for men, suggesting men might be underestimating how often this is happening.

This also rang true in the focus groups they ran, where women spoke of feeling 'duty bound' once a man had an erection for him to reach climax.[2] A 2018 survey of 7,000 women by Public Health England found that half of respondents aged between twenty-five and thirty-four did not enjoy their sex life.[3] When you've been socialised to believe that sex should prioritise keeping straight men happy, how do you counter that?

When I was twenty-six I made an attempt to speak up and was hit with a defensive rebuttal. I'd met him on a Friday night. It was the summer and Dora had gone to visit her friend in Berlin for the weekend. I was alone in the flat, sipping cheap red wine and scrolling through my Facebook news feed (it was 2017), which I'd planned to do until I fell asleep. I noticed a notification on my Messenger app and made the mistake of clicking on it. It was my uni boyfriend. He accused me of writing blogs about him on *gal-dem* because I was angry at him for personal reasons, not because I was trying to process his dubious views (at the time) on race. Rather than interrogate the ethics of memoir, the delicate negotiation between the right to write about your life and the feelings of people you could hurt, I sent a series of wine-stained messages telling him he was wrong: *how dare* he say my *little blogs* would come to nothing!! I texted a friend from school and asked if the invite to a house party in Hackney Wick, East London, was still open.

I arrived in the land of gentrified warehouses and it was soon a choice between the guy in question and the 'hat guy' (a guy standing by the DJ with a beanie on). 'The guy in question' was more forward, had chat and had cocaine, so he won. We went on a date or two. But when we had sex, there was never any foreplay. I didn't know what to do, so I consulted some group chats for advice.

'Expect to get some "home truths" in response if you do say something,' my friend Claire warned. She was right. 'You're not that good either,' he told me.

Now wait a minute – I have never professed to be good at sex. I am distinctly average at it. I don't mean this in a self-deprecating sense. I don't believe this was the intention of the sex-positivity movement, but it has not left much space to own sexual mediocrity. So I will try and own it now; I don't have it enough to list it in my top ten talents – it was true then and it is true now. All I'd asked this guy for was a warm-up before, you know, sticking it in. It's not about either of us being the best or knowing everything. Somewhere along the line though, that's the narrative we'd been sold. We needed to be great at sex and able to perform on cue or we're failures. The shame wasn't from being sexual but from either not having it often or it being average when it did. I had read enough articles and watched enough TV shows, so I knew what to do – end it, of course. They call it 'dump him' feminism for a reason. I felt like a no-nonsense fighter of patriarchy, a warrior who stood up for her needs. Now, I play it back and all I see is a young man who, in that moment, felt vulnerable and in response became defensive.

It's hard enough to know what you need, let alone to communicate it. And I wasn't having sex very often these days, although it took a while to figure out why.

In my early to mid-twenties, there was always a party or club night, with some hot gossip or salacious drama not too far behind it. It was effortless. We had a Facebook group called 'Nights Out – London'. I was out every weekend, me, my bare midriff, and shorts so short the pockets hung languid and visible, poking out the bottom. I moved bank account provider so I could pocket the £100 joining fee and use it to pay for a festival I couldn't afford. I lay drunkenly in the middle of road screaming: 'I just want to meet someone who sees me exactly as I am and IT'S ENOUGH!' just because some guy fancied someone else more than he fancied me. It meant I met people organically and with minimal effort. I used dating apps a little, but not all that much. But as I entered my late twenties, this began to happen less and less. We had formed close friendship groups and started to meet less new people. There were fewer and fewer friends of friends to be casually introduced to. The parties shrivelled as we aged. I was no longer habitually around new people. So sex became sporadic for me. I had one, undefined situationship* with someone I met through a friend. Outside of that – drought. Dryness, barren land, tumbleweeds.

A year and a half later, I'm back in Hackney. I'm having sex again (finally). It's the December of 2018 and I'm twenty-seven, although on the precipice of twenty-eight, and lying on a mattress with no bedframe in a studio space in Hackney Downs. My eyes focus on a spot on the ceiling, holding my gaze steady as if I'm trying to hold tree pose at a yoga studio. I'd met a guy in a club, in Hackney Wick, again, who had rushed to stick it in without foreplay. I couldn't stop thinking about my coat. It was winter and I had left it in a bar in Dalston. It's cold outside, I thought, I'm going to be very cold heading home. It might be worth waiting until the bar opens and getting it back before heading back to South London. I didn't know how to be confident and assertive with a stranger. I didn't know shit about sex. I didn't know anything about anything. The only thing I knew how to do was leave. So I did.

The next day my thrush was back.

I decided I was going to take matters into my own hands. I could train myself to pick better partners, get better at sex, and get better at communicating with effort and grit. I would be

* Situationship (noun) is a romantic relationship that's undefined or uncommitted. It may be based on convenience or short-term circumstances. It often has some or even all the trappings of a regular relationship, but without 'labels', commitment or direction. Word such as 'chill' normally used to describe them when 'no clarity' or 'confused' would be more accurate.

intentional. With the encouragement of a group of very motivated and inspirational black women, I made a list in my iPhone Notes app outlining my plans for the year ahead:

30 December 2018

I will be sexually liberated and fulfilled
Better sex/hoeation [being promiscuous, think Mary J Blige's 'hateration', its own genre of word] – be clearer about needs
OkCupid
Attend more parties/events with new people

This sat alongside other aspirational goals including:

Meditation
Yoga
Swimming [lessons]
Regular holidays – New York/Nigeria/Paris/Berlin
Set boundaries and say no more
Cut nonsense friends
Therapist
Twitter detox
Cooking

That same evening I went to a sex club, further cementing my new attitude. It meant I had to leave the vision board and goal-setting session early. I was nervous about giving the real reason I had to go, but when I shared it, I got full support. For all its limitations, sex-positivity has carved out space to be sexually up-for-it, to try new things outside of the norm of the heterosexual monogamous couple, and not be judged for it. And although I had imbibed a lot of lessons on sex from pop culture, mostly TV shows centred on four white female friends living in New York, that landscape had changed too. Now there was the TV show *Insecure* and the blogger and podcaster Oloni's infamous Twitter threads.

Naturally, I felt awkward at a sex club, standing nearly naked in the same South London nightclub I'd celebrated my eighteenth birthday at (was I a cool eighteen-year-old or a tragic twenty-seven-year-old?). But I was open to trying things and seeing where they would lead. In January 2019, I wrote a *gal-dem* column declaring it so, to hold myself publicly accountable.

It semi worked. I had sex six times that year, which was (sadly) a significant increase. I put myself out there and took risks. I went on a bad date with a guy from the sex club. I went to a themed 'dating experience'. I learnt that a room full of people who are as desperately single as you are, but without the pretence of a nightclub or a wedding, is un-British. It's too earnest and we're too awkward. Your cover at clubs, weddings and parties comes easily. You're there to 'have a dance' or 'celebrate love' and anything else is a treat, like getting one of those free coffees at Pret. I love fancy dress, a theme, and an orgy of organised fun. But dating relies on the pretence of mystery. It is the bicarbonate of soda of dating – without it, everything deflates. You couldn't speak to anyone who you didn't fancy, because, if you did, they thought you were chatting them up. It reminded me of the sex club.

We'd made a group chat ahead of the event with my then-colleagues (now proper friends). The next day, the friend I went with posted a direct quote from me in the chat:

'I went to [name of sex club] and this is worse' – Kim

I reinstalled dating apps and didn't feel emotionally wrecked by rejection. I had a one-night stand and enjoyed it. I swayed on the train from Camden to Denmark Hill, north to south, changed clothes and rocked up late to work.

I'd found a comfortable middle ground to lie on. Sex could be great, good, average and bad. It could be with the same person lots of times or a one-off, or with more than one person at the same time. It could be at home or at a sex club. It could be just because I could, because I felt like shaking things up after the rut of routine that accompanies getting older set in. Or it could be because I really liked someone and the sex feels like a mutual compulsion, a visceral urge you both share. It could be love.

If I'm honest, I don't know what I want from sex and definitely not how to ask for it. I don't how to make it better and I'm still distinctly average at it. I know I miss the whimsy, the excitement of my twenties when every night was an open question. But I don't miss the validation I sought from those encounters, which I've found in other, more concrete ways. My life has slowed down. When people ask me about my 'love life' and there is no update, I feel a sense of failure not because I am unhappy but because I don't have a story. I'm actively trying to push past this, that feeling that I'm losing precious time. That I should be on dating apps, precipitating a search for a hook-up or a partner, when right now at least, it doesn't feel like a priority that's come from me. It's an external message about how I should live. That the way I'm living is boring or that I'm being left behind. But sex, and any way I have it, isn't about a story that signals that I'm interesting, adventurous or cool. It's not even about knowing exactly what I want. It's about intimacy and vulnerability.

9 My teens and twenties told primarily through our Facebook updates

29 December 2006

Kimberly McIntosh updated her profile picture

Kimberly McIntosh edited her Home Town, Interests and Interested In

29 January 2007

Kimberly McIntosh updated her status:

Nearly 16!!!

2 February 2007

Kimberly McIntosh updated her status:

16!!!

4 March 2007

Kimberly McIntosh updated her status:

loving wireless internet

Josephine Clarke (Josie) wrote on your timeline:

snap on loving wireless internet btw!

28 March 2007

Dominic Sutton wrote on your timeline:

Sup kim. 2 hours ago, i was an msn-only guy lol – now look at me! facebook is weird at first but it looks better than shitty bebo. Trying to jump-start revision lol.

9 July 2007

Claire Jones wrote on your timeline:

no not much went 2a Justin Timberlake concert in the millennium dome which was amaaazing!! Fergie and Timberland (sic) were warm ups!!

29 July 2007

Kimberly McIntosh updated her status:

Shitting herself about 23 August!

18 August 2007

Susie Graham wrote on your timeline:

hey wanna teach me how to use this thing? i'm slightly confused lol xxx

23 August 2007

Kimberly McIntosh updated her status:

bloody excited about Reading festival and chuffed with her grades!

17 September 2007

Kimberly McIntosh updated her status:

Blaming Facebook and Perezhilton.com for her incomplete history essay

1 October 2007

Rachel Norton wrote on your timeline:

Kim!! how much do you think you'll write for your essay? Xxx

21 March 2008

Kimberly McIntosh updated her status:

Out of hospital for 4 days! Whoop Whoop!

10 July 2008

Kimberly McIntosh updated her status:

is watching some quality Jeremy Kyle

5 November 2008

Kimberly McIntosh updated her status:

loves High School Musical 3 and is loving Obama

21 December 2008

Kimberly McIntosh updated her status:

loves laserquest & is listening to Kanye while trying to ease a self inflicted headache.

24 December 2008

Kimberly McIntosh updated her status:

Queued 2 hours for Revs* but it was worth it for Vodka Touch!

24 December 2008

Adam Brown wrote on your timeline:

LOVE YOU KIM XXXX happy xmas

* A chain nightclub called Revolution that is a staple of provincial towns across the UK.

<u>**16 January 2009**</u>
Kimberly McIntosh updated her status:
is the female version of a hustler

<u>**30 January 2009**</u>
Kimberly McIntosh updated her status:
CAN DRINK, VOTE AND DANCE

<u>**25 March 2009**</u>
Kimberly McIntosh updated her status:
is go baby go baby, GO! Don't upset the rhythm

<u>**5 April 2009**</u>
Kimberly McIntosh updated her status:
Wants to go back in time, slap Wordsworth and Coleridge around the face, and order them to never write poetry – especially about nature. ERGH!

<u>**29 May 2009**</u>
Kimberly McIntosh updated her status:
Head hurts after 6 hours of Wordsworth and WWI literature ☹

<u>**30 May 2009**</u>
Kimberly McIntosh updated her status:
Another day, more WWI, ERGH!

<u>**7 June 2009**</u>
Kimberly McIntosh updated her status:
ERGH, the BNP* have two seats and I have a 3 hour exam, what a week this is turning out to be!

* British National Party, a far-right, fascist political party in the UK that had some electoral success in the early 2000s.

16 July 2009

Kimberly McIntosh updated her status:

Wishes the piece of shit that is my Blackberry would bloody work

20 August 2009

Kimberly McIntosh updated her status:

HEAVY DRINKING TONIGHT – Manchester 2010!!! See you at Revs party people 😮

20 October 2009

Kimberly McIntosh updated her status:

is hanging so bad . . . time for round two at Sakura tonight!

3 February 2010

Kimberly McIntosh updated her status:

last Revs Tuesday: End of an era

9 February 2010

Kimberly McIntosh updated her status:

10 hours until our flight to Rio!!!!!!

24 March 2010

Kimberly McIntosh updated her status:

is glad Argentinian nightlife doesn't start until 2am . . . plenty of time to indulge in Jersey Shore tonight without guilt

5 April 2010

Kimberly McIntosh updated her status:

Spent Saturday night trying to explain in broken Spanglish what a 'Sexy Bitch' is

20 June 2010

Kimberly McIntosh updated her status:

Drunk in Costa Rica!!!!!! 2.50 for unlimited drinks, awesome night

25 June 2010

Kimberly McIntosh updated her status:

Allow football, I'm coming home

22 October 2010

Kimberly McIntosh updated her status:

Did not enjoy the 4am fire alarm. Or 7am repeat. Livid.

18 October 2010

Kimberly McIntosh updated her status:

First article in the student paper!

7 November 2010

Kimberly McIntosh updated her status:

On the way home to Manchester with clean laundry

10 November 2010

Kimberly McIntosh updated her status:

wishes I had skived lectures and hit up the protest!*

24 November 2010

Kimberly McIntosh updated her status:

was scared shitless when the police charged at us with horses and wishes they would let us go home!**

* The 2010 student protests in London against the proposed university fee hike from approximately £3,000 per year to £9,000 per year, https://www.vice.com/en/article/qjddzb/oral-history-2010-student-protests

** One of the Manchester-based student protests in 2010 against university fee hikes. Heavy police presence.

<u>**30 November 2010**</u>

Kimberly McIntosh updated her status:

why is there a trolley in my room?

<u>**8 December 2010**</u>

Kimberly McIntosh updated her status:

Is rich!!! Hello 900 pound bursary

Day 9 of drinking before my Spanish exam, not dumb at all . . .

<u>**12 December 2010**</u>

Kimberly McIntosh updated her status:

Wants this essay done so the carnage can begin

10 Twenty-four-hour party people

I am an unapologetic drug user. I take drugs as part of my pursuit of happiness, and they work. I am a happier and better person because of them. I am also a scientist and a professor of psychology specialising in neuroscience at Columbia University, known for my work on drug abuse and addiction.[1]

Dr Carl Hart, *Drug Use for Grown Ups: Chasing Liberty in the Land of Fear.*

If you want to get to the heart of the dope problem, legalize it. That destroys the profit motive, and may save our children. [Prohibition] is a law, which in operation can be used only against the poor.[2]

James Baldwin, keynote speech, National Press Club luncheon, 10 December 1986.

In my senior year of college I swallowed MDMA for the first time with a friend who showed up with a bag of like 100 pills. I took one. Within an hour, it felt like the world was made of pleasure, that my bones were shivering miracles. I remember thinking in the moment that maybe sex was supposed to feel like this, but I hadn't met that level of lover yet.[3]

adrienne maree brown, *Pleasure Activism: The Politics of Feeling Good.*

It was the summer of 2011 and I was a recent convert to the cult of *3,4-Methylenedioxymethamphetamine*, aka MDMA or Ecstasy. I approached drugs at university with caution. I treated them with more care than losing my virginity. Sex was cool and for the thriving. Drugs, I had believed, were for the foolish.

I'd learnt these hard facts in primary school, where all of life's dangers were taught via VHS on a big telly that was inexplicably on wheels. This particular video was about the dangers of sniffing glue. I don't remember much, but my flatmate and I (who also recalls a similar video from her school days, 200 miles up the M6) are pretty sure there was a disused train track and that it may have also doubled up as a video about the dangers of pylons. Another friend's drug education consisted solely of her biology teacher's husband – a local policeman – coming into a PSHE lesson and telling the class he'd found three teens dead behind a shed, all because of glue. That was it. I got another dose of scare tactics in the form of some traumatising, graphic photographs of teenagers in dire straits and a talk where a girl came in and told us how drugs had ruined her life.

The message was clear: 'hard' drugs were for the teens already descending the slippery highway to hell via the gateways of glue, cigarettes and cannabis. Controlled substances (illegal drugs) were for models and pop stars; normal people became addicts or died on the spot. Obviously, alcohol was fine because it's legal. By my mid-teens I'd dabbled with boozing on rare occasions in the park. We got into a dodgy bar (since closed) where I threw up Malibu and lay down in the doorway before being coaxed into a cab to a friend's place. Then we found that one restaurant that would serve us in town (since closed), and that working men's social club/bar/pub that would serve anyone (since closed), until I finally turned eighteen.

I wanted to try alcohol when I was underage because there was a thrill to doing something that I wasn't meant to. I continued to drink once I was legally allowed to because it's fun. Alcohol is psychoactive, meaning it affects the brain and as a result can change your consciousness, mood, behaviour and perceptions.[4] Humans have the desire to alter their minds with substances and that desire is not new. Sometimes it is practical. Most offices have tea and coffee making stations because caffeine, a psychoactive substance aka a drug, is a stimulant that can make us feel more awake. Or drugs can have cultural or spiritual associations, like communities chewing the coca leaf in the Andes or taking ayahuasca with a shaman in the Amazon.[5] For better or worse, drinking in the pub is a cornerstone of British culture, used to socialise and build community, to fight boredom during winter, to celebrate sporadic heatwaves in summer, to obscure emotions, feel less inhibited and to forget.

But when we talk about *drugs*, we generally don't mean caffeine, alcohol, cigarettes or even ayahuasca: we mean cocaine, Ecstasy, heroin and weed. When we were taught about drugs in school, those were the drugs I associated with 'no hopers' and that's not an accident.

'If you talked about a "drugs problem" 200 years ago, no one would have known what you meant. There was no notion of "drugs"', wrote the historian of medicine Roy Porter in 1996.[6] Plants such as opium (that can be used to make heroin) and coca (that can be used to make cocaine) were commodities, which, alongside tea and tobacco and spirits like rum, created great wealth for the British, Dutch and French empires.[7]

In the nineteenth century, drugs of all kinds were widely available in the UK. Some of the stalwarts of my GCSE English Literature classes – Samuel Taylor Coleridge, Lord Byron and Charles Dickens – were mad for opium and its influence laces their stanzas and sentences.[8] Cocaine and opium were both legal in Britain up until the First World War.[9]

In the late nineteenth century, anti-vice campaigners in the US started linking particular drugs with minoritised ethnic groups in an attempt to fortify their campaigns. Chinese migrants became 'opium fiends', African-American men were cocaine hounds 'imbued with superhuman strength' and Mexican communities were associated with the 'epidemic' of cannabis-fuelled 'wild orgies' and 'debauchery' by using the Spanish-sounding term marijuana. All of these groups were posed as a 'threat' to white women.[10] Drugs as we know them today began to take on moral meanings and an international movement for global drug prohibition gained momentum. Cannabis, opium and coca shapeshifted, no longer commodities to be traded but phantasmic substances that according to the 1961 United Nations Single Convention on Narcotic Drugs were a 'social and economic danger for mankind'.[11] The Convention aimed to combat drug consumption by limiting the possession, consumption and trade of illegal drugs globally.[12] Tragically, this Convention, the bedrock on which the War on Drugs was built, spearheaded by US president Richard Nixon in the 1970s and embraced in the 1980s by Ronald Reagan and British Prime Minister Margaret Thatcher, has led to increases in accidental overdoses, mass incarceration, extreme violence, millions dead and destroyed livelihoods across continents. Yet drug consumption remains buoyant and the trade thriving.[13]

Under pressure from Washington, the Drugs (Regulation of Misuse) Act 1964 was passed in the UK, giving power to the police to search people, particularly young black men or black teenage children, for illicit drugs and make them subject to criminal sentences. This was updated in 1971 to become the Misuse of Drugs Act. This is the same legislation we still have today – over fifty years on. Britain is in many ways a socially conservative country. But in fifty years we've managed to formally outlaw racial discrimination in public spaces, housing and employment via three pieces of legislation. Women can no longer be fired for being pregnant. There are laws on equal pay, gender pay gaps and marriage equality. Yet drug policy remains a fossil, perfectly preserved but useless in the present for anything other than as a relic. It's like trying to write this essay on an Apple-1 computer, being surprised when it continually crashes, and doggedly refusing to buy a readily available MacBook. Rather than basing the law on the facts – how much a drug can cause harm to the person using it and the people they care for – it's based on arbitrary categories and moral panics. It allows alcohol companies to advertise to us with abandon on TV and in train stations but buries the trade for cannabis underground.

So I arrived at Manchester University believing binge drinking was normal because it is not only legal but practically a national pastime. I was very anti-drugs and only had abstinence-based drug education to my name. Useful methods for scaring teenagers away from drugs they do not need; useless tools that do nothing to prepare you for university where drugs are, in fact, very cool. So when I eventually caved and tried to inhale a spliff to impress a guy in our block, I couldn't do it. I coughed manically, the smoke and my ill-fitting side fringe conspiring to expose me as sheltered and painfully uncool. My flatmates made weed brownies instead so I could be included and the only consequence was that I slept for twelve hours and had to wear sunglasses to the pub. So the rules I'd allowed to govern my life unquestioned lost their rigidity. I wasn't famous and yet here I was, very much alive.

Months after the brownie, I experienced a great betrayal. The flat below went to an illegal rave under a motorway bridge without me and took MDMA for the first time. They didn't knock-on because I had freshers' flu and they had to act fast to not miss their lift, apparently. To this day, I have not forgiven them.* They would not stop going on about how cool it was and how great this drug was.

I was caught between two conflicting parts of my personality. I'd always been a cautious person who worried a lot. Then, at seventeen, I caught tuberculosis and was hospitalised. No one knows where I got it from and the doctors told me it will forever remain a medical mystery. Thinking I might die, ending my life

* That's right, babs – I will never forget! You know who you are!!!

a risk-averse virgin felt tragic. I wanted to experience everything, even when it frightened me. But MDMA was a 'hard' drug, which felt extra risky. So I considered the evidence for and against taking *3,4-Methylenedioxymethamphetamine*, or Mandy as we called it in 2010. I pored over a British National Formulary book, a pharmaceutical reference book with information and advice on pharmacology (safety first). Like my friend had done with her virginity in school, I chose the perfect place (the big end of year party), I rejected any offers before this specific date (turning down free cocaine a week before) and I prepared my body and mind for my first time (one beer and the right amount of water).

Anyone new to narcotics needs a drug shepherd – someone who grew up in a big city, attended a large college, or went to a really elite private school and had consequently taken drugs before university – ready to lead the flock. Luckily, our block had a friendly neighbourhood drug dealer, another student who lived in the flat below mine. Student dealer had the gentle, lo-fi manner common to stoners – slow movements, soft gestures and a cloud of weed smoke that hung on him casually like an oversized accessory. He would only sell me one-eighth of a gram of MDMA, rather than the standard half a gram you might take out with you. 'You've never done it before and you're small. You will not need more than that,' he told me.

He is now in jail, sentenced to fifteen years for conspiracy to import, export and supply controlled drugs. Three other students were also sentenced.[14] Their operation was intercepted by the FBI and, on arrest, their sales were at least £812,000.

On 9 June 2011, I took MDMA for the first time. From then on, some of the best and the worst of times will be marshalled by illegal drugs. I'll be brave enough to text that guy. I'll write what I believe to be life-changing prose in my Notes app then wake to realise it's trash. I'll enter a mental state so vivid I am convinced I'll be stuck there forever and demand my friends let me call a psychologist at 4 a.m.

My friends and I will spend years stumbling through the dark – the dingy basements, the stylised warehouses, the hills of the Peak District and that famous farm in Somerset – grasping desperately for some guidance on drug taking – how to get them and take them safely. When we found none, we tried our best to make it up.

Our student dealers will take us on a big night out and pay for everything. Then they'll fall off the map until I read about their prison sentences in the papers.[15] I'll watch black men be stopped and searched, one by one, in a scattered line on 4/20*, while I waltz into Hyde Park, white friends in tow, bras and socks stuffed with weed, all unscathed. But the drug I find the hardest to control, and the one that will put me in the most danger time and time again, is alcohol.

• • •

The first time I take MDMA I'm dressed as an elephant. I'm covered in silver paint everywhere except my face, so I still look pretty in photos. I put the powder on my gums and water begins to pool in the pockets of my mouth, the prelude to throwing up. No one has warned me about the taste. Thirty or so minutes pass, and with them, years of being tightly wound and highly strung unravel. I'm a rainbow slinky bounding down a spiral staircase in a blur of enthusiasm. A sputter of joy and colour.

Each room is a different take on the jungle. I have animated conversations as if I've been put on fast forward. There is a photo I have since removed from the internet where, eyes wide and grinning, I look like a silver Cheshire Cat with fake eyelashes. I blink, the eyelashes are askew and the night is over. The sun is

* On 20 April (4/20 in the US calendar, which is MM/DD instead of DD/MM), people gather to celebrate cannabis often by smoking it in public parks. https://www.vox.com/policy-and-politics/2019/4/19/18484698/what-is-420-meaning-marijuana-legalization

up. We all huddle on one single bed together. I'm all in, although I'll never feel that rush as intently again.

In *Trick Mirror: Reflections on Self-Delusion*, journalist Jia Tolentino compares the euphoria of MDMA with the spiritual homecoming she felt at her megachurch.[16] 'Ecstasy does not confuse the user about what is occurring,' she says. 'Your awareness of self and of basic reality remains unchanged.' This is what is so great about it – the lowering of inhibitions without the loss of memory or control that had come to shadow my experiences with alcohol. I love the involuntary truth telling; an acid reflux of cloying word vomit. There's nothing brave about telling your friends you love them when you're on MDMA, it's as if your emotions have been doused in MSG and all your latent feelings are brought out and enhanced. It's your beliefs and it's your serotonin, all just heightened with an additive.

My caution about drugs, instilled by the law and the scaremongering school talks, dissolved along with the powder, just a few fragments of it visible at the bottom of the pint glass.

I stayed until the bitter end of the semester that year. The last weeks of the final term were an endurance test in going *out out*; a bleep test that gets harder with each lap. On the final night out, the student dealer was bankrolling everything from taxis, to entry, to drinks. It was hip-hop night, I think. I may have been sick in the loo, although that could have been any other night. But I still remember how it ended. The student dealer got punched in the face, rumour has it, by a rival dealer. It was time to go home – from the club and for the summer. What goes up must come down is true of drugs and also of life. It was time to head back south to Reading, Berkshire.

The punching incident triggered the slow creep of more serious questions that, as hangovers do with each passing year, grow more intense and harder to shake off, like where do our drugs come from and what's in them?

Initially, where these drugs came from did not concern me.

It arrived at the campus post office from the dark web marketplace Silk Road, a part of the internet infamous for the anonymous buying and selling of illegal drugs and other unlawful goods and services. The drugs were then sold to us from the convenience of our block on the Fallowfield campus. But, in second year, we're not living in halls any more (the members of our block have graduated to the rickety house shares and multiple occupancy hellholes of Fallowfield, Withington and Didsbury, south Manchester) so getting the drugs becomes more complicated. The part of Fallowfield where our beautiful nine-bed nightmare sits is so notorious for its festival-like parties, it made the cut for a feature in the *Observer*. In 2018, local families confessed, on condition of anonymity, that the area had become 'party central' with gatherings that had: 'bouncers, guest lists, drug deliveries, DJs and business cards dropped all over the area with someone's first name, a number and a little sample of cannabis on them so you can call the dealer'.[17] Student heaven; family hell.

With the first Warehouse Project coming up, we needed to pick up some drugs. After asking around, a friend said the student dealers weren't doing small-time supplies any more. Rumour had it, that if you were their inner circle you could still access their burgeoning supply, the bricks of powders stacked up in their new home.

I didn't really know what the Silk Road was, let alone how to use it. And I wasn't even peripherally orbiting the inner circle. So I had to learn how to pick up drugs the old-fashioned way – off the street. The first time I had to text a drug dealer, I curated it with an arduous attention to detail.

'Will the dealer dish it up into eighths for me like [student dealer] did?' I asked our housemate, who had taken drugs before university.

'Are you fucking joking? No.'

'Can you send the text for me?'

'No. Grow up.'

I grow up and send the text. Something simple like:

Thu 17 Sept
19:27
Hey. Got your number from [redacted]. Can I get 2g of Mandy?

I've done it! I am brave.

I wear Jack Wills* skinny trackies tucked into Ugg boots and an American Eagle shirt for protection, based on my assumption that the police let preppy kids do whatever they want. As I walk down Edgerton Road, Fallowfield, I spot the inconspicuous black car with its engine still running. I get in, have some small talk, pay and leave. The drugs are no longer dished out for me into the precise portions I need with my safety in mind. And the quality of the drugs is questionable. One night, I think I've picked up ketamine but it feels different and we realise it's probably another illicit substance called MXE.

'If you were buying alcohol, you'd never go and buy 80 per cent proof if you were five foot one, and didn't drink very much,' Vicky Unwin, a leading member of Anyone's Child: Families for Safer Drug Control, told me. She lost her twenty-one-year-old daughter Louise in 2011, after she took ketamine with friends. '[Louise] weighed everything out, she was actually not stupid, you know? But they all had the same dose. And she was five foot one, and the other people were regular users, and were bigger.'

Admirably, Unwin has been an active campaigner on drug policy reform ever since. She not only raises awareness of the dangers and risks that come with taking ketamine but also advocates for its legalisation.

---

* This was the OG Jack Wills, before it's recent 'urban' rebrand. A desperate bid to stay relevant.

'I always said, I never wanted to see drugs banned, because I don't think that's a solution. It's like, you stop your kids drinking alcohol, they're gonna just go and get pissed round the back of the bike sheds. So let's just concentrate on telling people how to do it safely,' she said.

'If you regulate it, and you get it from a trusted source, you know what's in it. And if you want to take ketamine and be that stupid, well, at least you can get it from somewhere, and it's unlikely to kill you unless you take more than the prescribed dose. I think it would save a lot of lives.'

Unlike alcohol, there's no regulation to make sure illegal drugs are what we've been told they are. In the first year of uni, I used to buy alcohol from an iconic corner shop where wine only cost one pound and there was a vodka whose label would change periodically, given a new identity to escape detection as if it were in witness protection. Its acidic content stayed the same. In December that year, BBC news reported that 2,500 bottles of Aros/Drop Vodka/Arctic Ice had been seized by Trading Standards in a raid of an illegal vodka distillery.[18] We stopped drinking it and started buying Sainsbury's Basics vodka instead. Although its taste resembles paint thinner, at least you can guarantee it's not an illegal solvent. Silk Road at least had an eBay-like ratings and review system where customers would vouch for the quality of the seller's wares. I've even known of someone getting replacement product after the drugs that arrived turned out to be a placebo. There is no such system of shop-style customer service on the street and this can have catastrophic consequences.

In November 2013, seventeen attendees to the Warehouse Project were hospitalised after a batch of dodgy pills, thought to be Ecstasy, were sold and taken by punters. They had actually taken PMA, a drug that can have similar effects to MDMA but has a higher toxicity level. It takes a lot less of it to accidentally overdose and end up in hospital. It also takes longer to kick in, a potent double-bind which encourages users to take more of something that is in fact stronger. A thirty-year-old man died in hospital after taking it.[19]

'The issue is really that they don't know what they're taking. Whereas if you buy a can of Coke, you know pretty much that you're getting a can of Coke,' said Dr Steve Jones, who was in charge of emergency medicine at Manchester Royal Infirmary at the time.[20]

PMA had entered the supply chain as a direct result of the United Nations trying to *reduce* the prevalence of MDMA consumption. In 1999, they banned the precursor used to make MDMA at the time, safrole, an oil that's extracted from sassafras plants grown in tropical forests in China, and later in Cambodia. Large-scale seizures of the oil in 2007–2008 caused a global MDMA shortage.[21] To circumvent the ban, underground chemists started using aniseed oil instead, processing it in the same way they had with safrole. But instead of getting MDMA, they produced PMA or PMMA.[22] The chemists eventually found a workaround to make MDMA synthetically rather than from plants that, thankfully, didn't produce PMA. And as MDMA re-emerged, PMA deaths dropped.[23] The new process, however, made MDMA much stronger and cheaper. This is thought to have increased MDMA-related deaths, which rose by over 50 per cent between 2016 and 2018.[24]

Ending up in the emergency department is fortunately rare, suggesting most people have worked out how to use MDMA without experiencing severe harm.[25] The majority of people who use illegal drugs recreationally only use them occasionally and will not go on to develop problematic use, and often stop using them by their thirties. This is particularly true for drugs associated with going out or parties, like Ecstasy and cocaine, where over half of users in 2018–2019 had only used the drug once or twice in the year.[26] People take them because it's fun and much of the harm they cause to individuals is a result of not knowing what you're buying or how much to take in order to minimise risk.

Once I started taking illegal drugs at uni, there was no blueprint to help me navigate how to use them responsibly. The best surrogate was alcohol, which we've been socialised to consume at every occasion. When we win in life we celebrate with alcohol, and when we commiserate failure, trauma and tragedy, we drink even more. This is despite the fact that there is no other drug that is as damaging to so many organs in the body through toxicity alone as alcohol. Most drugs cause damage chiefly to one or two specific organs – alcohol is harmful almost everywhere.[27] So I started using illegal drugs the way I consumed alcohol: to celebrate and to socialise and to dance, but also at times to manage discomfort and sadness and to feel more confident.

The best of times on illegal drugs: 2011–2016

54 house party (2011)

Our flat hosts a house party just because. It doesn't have a bouncer but it does have DJs in the downstairs kitchen. The upstairs kitchen is for smoking and there's a mattress taking up most of the 'living room' area, where guests can chill out and chat. I go to the bathroom and three guys I've never met are racking lines of coke on the cistern.

'Who the fuck are you?!' one of them asks.

'I fucking live here.'

'Wheeeyyy,' they say in unison and then offer me some cocaine.

I accidentally blow out instead of in, the powder escaping the well-ordered lines like a toddler's early attempts at colouring. They forgive the schoolboy error, put it neatly back in a line, and give me a second go. It works, and one of the guys says, with an elegant wave of the hand: 'And that, my love, is cocaine.'

I'm finally living my teenage fantasy: *Skins* but without all the trauma!

Outlook & Dimensions Festival (2012)

Beaches! Music! Stages! Drugs! Our friend gets us onto a boat party. We get free T-shirts and 'Another Girl' by Jacques Greene, my favourite song at the time, plays as we board. My headband matches my bikini and my hair has fallen naturally into curls from sweat and sea spray. The sun beams on us and we drift along the Adriatic Sea. I know one of my friends will bang the DJ but it's unclear which one will prevail. I live for the drama.

Sunrise on the roof in Toronto (2012)

It's the end of the semester at the University of Toronto, where Mandy is called Molly and is sold out of a frat house called Delta Kappa Epsilon. One of the student co-ops where my friends live is having a party. As the party is slowing down and winding up, some of us get up on the roof and watch the sunrise.

Pangea with Grandmaster Flash (2013)

It's my twenty-second birthday! Taylor Swift has released the song called '22', about feeling twenty-two, which feels apt, as I'm also twenty-two!! I'm dressed as a giant playing card and Grandmaster Flash is the headliner. I run into a girl from primary school in the bathroom. Life is random like that and that's what makes it beautiful (+ the MDMA helps).

Free party in Peak District (2013)

A controversial politician who is deeply unpopular in some segments of northern England and Wales dies. A party happens to be thrown in the Peak District on that same day. It may or may not have caused the outraged *Daily Mail* headline: 'Major clean-up at National Park beauty spot after 2,000 Death Party ravers leave trail of destruction'.[28] I mostly remember the sense that all parties are best when they're free, climbing onto a giant speaker and that most people took their litter home with them.

Sunrise on the roof at the final party after Parklife Festival (2013)

I love a sunrise that is also a metaphorical marker of new beginnings and change! We're graduating and moving on. We come down and the sun comes up (isn't the symmetry of life + MDMA magical?). It's time to move from Manchester to London.

My friend [redacted]'s parties (2016)

A friend used to throw iconic fancy-dress parties once or twice a year. The theme was taken very seriously, with structures built to transform their house and garden into outer space or the sea or the underworld. In 2016, I am the rainbow fish from the children's book, *The Rainbow Fish*, and successfully use a Numark DJ controller in front of people for the first time. People dance and sing along as I play songs! I've just discovered Kaytranada. I shag some guy who claims to be a musician and is horrified to find out I cannot play any musical instruments and am 'not actually, like, *that* into music'.

The worst of times on illegal drugs (2011–2015)

Taking Ecstasy at a party because I'm upset (2011)

I found out I was implicated in someone cheating on their girlfriend because he failed to mention he had one. I feel terrible but I won't for long if I take Ecstasy!

Mushroom incident in Amsterdam (2011)

I'm trapped with four friends and a thousand judgemental hipsters (OK, only four to five judgemental hipsters), the friends of friends of my flatmates from Brighton. One night in our shitty hostel, we take magic mushrooms and I don't cotton on that because I'm only five foot I should probably take less than the rest of the group, who are all taller. Initially, I'm a balloon that is tied to the ground, or, to any sober onlooker, a twenty-year-old on mushrooms who is standing on one leg by *Café The Doors* on Singel

14. In another café, a snakeskin countertop sets me off into a spiral of despair. In another, I ruminate in the shadows of my subconscious, while a friend comforts me.

The aftermath of Outlook & Dimensions Festival (2012)

The cumulative comedown from two festivals, no sleep (just adrenaline and vibes), junk food, day drinking, drama, my Ray-Bans and high-top trainers being stolen, a delayed flight, the coach from a nonsense airport like Stansted to London Victoria, and the first a.m. train from Paddington to Reading was ferocious. I land in my bed on the brink of tears.

Glastonbury 2C-B incident *(2015)*

Glastonbury is fabulous as is 2C-B, a synthetic drug with psychedelic effects. The impact of 2C-B, however, is heavily dose-dependent and, as with the mushrooms in Amsterdam incident, I take the same as everyone else instead of a tiny bit. Initially, the lights around the festival start to glow more intensely, blurring slightly before coming into focus again as if they are beating or breathing to a rhythm. I talk with a friend about my relationship with religion as we walk. Then as I'm lying down in the tent attempting to sleep my mind turns in on itself. The vivid colours and visions that were light and enjoyable are now invasive. I close my eyes and there are permanent patterns like intrusive thoughts I can't blink away. I'm scared I'll be trapped in overstimulation forever and my friends have to stop me from calling another friend who's doing a master's in Psychology because I NEED a psychologist otherwise I'll be stuck here FOREVER. It is 4 a.m. and he is not at the festival. Eventually, I fall asleep.

All of these events – our student cul-de-sac riddled with the house parties, the festivals and nights out – are saturated with drug use. But they are only superficially policed.

• • •

Taking drugs at university, at music festivals and at house parties is as ground-breaking as florals for spring. But drugs are policed differently depending on who's presumed to be taking them and who's delivering them.

In summer 2016 I attend two large-scale events that are policed very differently. One is the festival Secret Garden Party, described by *Vice* journalist Tshepo Mokoena as an escapist fantasy for middle-class kids. Its founder Freddie Fellowes is an old Etonian, an heir to a £35 million fortune, and the son of John Ailwyn Fellowes, the fourth Baron de Ramsey.[29] The other is Notting Hill Carnival, Europe's biggest street party and the unapologetic celebration of the music, food and culture of the Caribbean diaspora. It was founded by the Trinidadian activist, editor and dedicated communist, Claudia Jones, in 1959.[30]

Secret Garden Party was an immersive festival that, in honour of its posh roots, was big on fancy dress. The theme in 2016 is a 'Gardeners' Guide to the Galaxy', aka space shit. I don my Pinterest-inspired outfit, a Boohoo barely-there backless crop top with a sun and moon on it, silver leggings and a headband that resembles a galaxy mobile you might attach to a baby's cot. Like the work of a child trying to recreate something they've watched on *Art Attack*, it doesn't quite look like the one on my screen that someone made earlier, but I tried my best. I pull on my obligatory Hunter wellies, even though the forecast on BBC Weather is four straight days of suns, and board a train to Cambridgeshire.

Nearly everyone on the train is heading to the festival. I sit diagonally across the aisle from an old white man who is enraptured in conversation with three white girls in revealing clothing and an explosion of glitter. They are explaining the festival to him. He makes sure to punctuate the conversation by taking frequent breaks to glare at me. So I take out a copy of *Revolutionary Suicide*, the autobiography of American Black Panther Huey P. Newton, and performatively read it for the remainder of the journey. The cover art is an illustration of Huey with the signature black beret on his head, the police in the distance behind him, and a gun pressed against his neck. The glare intensifies.

2016 was the penultimate year of the festival and the first year it deployed a pioneering harm-reduction approach to drug use. In collaboration with the not-for-profit company The Loop, they ran the Multi Agency Safety Testing (MAST) programme that allowed festival-goers to submit samples of their drugs for testing and ascertain their content, purity and strength without any police interference. It was supported by the local authority, local public health authorities and the police.[31] Professor Fiona Measham, co-founder of The Loop, said that having experienced drug workers, testing and tailored advice can reduce risks and save lives.[32]

The drug testers found that one in five substances sold at SGP were not as described by dealers. There were samples that contained ketamine instead of cocaine, while a drug sold as MDMA turned out to be n-ethylpentylone, a long-lasting drug that can cause anxiety, paranoia, insomnia and psychosis. Two-thirds of people who discovered they had had substances mis-sold to them subsequently handed them to the police.[33] While festival drug-related deaths in England and Wales reached their highest on record that year, there was only one drug-related hospital admission at SGP, down from nineteen the previous year.[34] The combination of collaborative policing and a public health approach, which sees drug users as patients, not criminals, saved lives.

'There are still discussions around harm reduction, because some countries think you are incentivising people to use drugs – that's not the case,' Dr João Goulão told me from the Portuguese capital, Lisbon. Portugal took a harm reduction and risk minimisation approach to illegal drugs in 1999, when Goulão led a panel of nine experts, from judges to psychiatrists, to create Portugal's first comprehensive drug strategy. It was passed by Parliament in 2001, and famously meant the possession and consumption of illicit substances was no longer a criminal offence. 'I do not criminalise someone who eats lots of sugar because he's diabetic. I do not put [him] in jail because he drinks alcohol. But I do try to offer health responses and get [him] some treatment.'

Someone caught with a small amount of illegal drugs will have them confiscated by the police, but instead of facing criminal penalties, they may get a fine and will also be sent to a panel that includes health professionals and social workers. They can then assess the individual's relationship to drugs, and whether they need any support. If, say, a young person comes in and has been smoking weed recreationally, but is having struggles in their personal life – their parents are divorcing or they are struggling with their gender identity – they will be offered therapy, for free. 'We understood from the very beginning . . . we could not get people to not find [drugs] if they wanted that. We want to avoid these drug users [becoming] more problematic users later on,' Goulão told me.

Notting Hill Carnival is a much larger event than Secret Garden Party with a wider target audience. For Carnival, I have a feather headdress in place of the homemade space mobile contraption on my head, my obligatory Jamaican flag and my green horn. But as a free event in central London that celebrates Caribbean culture, it draws a more diverse crowd, and certainly more black people than SGP. Or as I overheard two white people describe the Carnival on the Tube a few years ago: 'It's like their [black people's] Christmas.' An estimated 1.5 million revellers descended on Notting Hill over 2 days in 2016. Secret Garden Party had about 30,000 people over 4 days. At SGP, we took MDMA at least once a day. At Carnival we drank alcohol.

As SGP got praise for its pioneering public health approach to drug taking and collaborative policing, a different approach was used to police Notting Hill Carnival. A combination of tactics, including high visibility policing (lots of uniformed and plain clothed police officers), pre-emptive raids, riot policing and policing with detection dogs, was used to manage the event. Over 6,000 Met officers were deployed at Carnival on the Sunday and nearly 7,000 on the Monday.[35] In a report on the future of the

Carnival written that year, former Conservative London Assembly Member and then-Chair of the Police and Crime Committee Steve O'Connell said that 'unfortunately, the positives associated with Carnival are overshadowed each year by the level of crime that is reported to take place'.[36]

In 2016, there were 454 arrests at Carnival. That's a mere 0.03 per cent of attendees arrested for crime. And out of those 454 arrests, only 227 were for drug offences (including nitrous oxide or laughing gas, which became illegal to sell for consumption that year, causing confusion).[37] Conversely, if we scale the crowd up to match that of Carnival, Secret Garden Party had 1,600 drug-related arrests that same year. And as Patrick Heardman explains for *Vice*, Latitude Festival, 'voted best family friendly festival in the 2012 UK Festival Awards' – the same festival where my friend and I spotted a woman holding her baby in one arm while using her free hand to do a key of a white powder – had double the number of drug-related arrests as Carnival did.[38]

Notting Hill Carnival has other challenges for the police to consider, such as global terrorism threats and increasing knife crime.[39] Preventing violent crime from happening at Carnival is important for both the safety of guests and the event's reputation. But to claim that the level of crime overshadows the positives of the event is anchored in prejudice.

Although drug arrests are proportionally larger at other music events, this doesn't stop the Metropolitan Police from publicly making the link between drug crime and Carnival anyway. In August 2017, five days before Notting Hill Carnival, the Met tweeted:

> In the run up to #NottingHillCarnival, officers have this morning seized what is believed to be a kilo of uncut heroin in #Catford.[40]

Twitter users were quick to note that Catford is twelve miles away from Notting Hill, over an hour's drive. And is there really a huge heroin market at Carnival? Grime artist Stormzy took to Twitter to ask how many drugs were seized 'in the run up to Glastonbury or we only doing tweets like this for black events?'[41]

The Met have since deleted the tweet. But the belief that black people are more likely to be involved in drug taking and selling goes beyond the over-policing of black parties. It also extends to the over-policing of black lives more generally. Black and Asian people consistently report much lower rates of taking drugs compared to white people, especially the supposedly 'harder' Class A ones like cocaine and Ecstasy. In the government's *Crime Survey for England and Wales* in 2016/2017, black respondents reported using cannabis at about half the rate of white people, and Class A drugs at less than quarter the rate of white people.[42]

I have only been stopped once ever in my life, protected by a combination of class (the places I go are either not policed or superficially so) and my gender (which positions me as less of a 'threat'). This isn't a privilege everyone has. The Child Q case, an appalling strip-search of a black fifteen-year-old at her East London school in 2020, is a prime example. She was taken out of an exam by two female Metropolitan police officers who were looking for cannabis. No one contacted her parents, her sanitary towel was removed and no drugs were found. A safeguarding report found that racism was 'likely' to have been a factor and the search was unjustified.[43] This would never have happened at my suburban private school.

So while I spent 2016–2017 gallivanting from party to party, criss-crossing the country to festivals and smoking weed in Hyde Park on 4/20, black people were being stopped and searched for drugs at 8.7 times the rate of white people in England and Wales.[44]

The difference in treatment could perhaps be justified if black people were more likely to deal drugs. Preventing violent crimes, particularly knife crime, is also used as a justification for increasing stop and search. But even though black people are stopped disproportionately, they're less likely than white people to be found actually carrying drugs when they're stopped. Put another way, black people – mostly men – are being harassed. Her Majesty's Inspectorate of Constabulary and Fire and Rescue Services (HMICFRS), the emergency services watchdog, called the practice 'one of the most intrusive powers available to the police' and noted it's 'becoming increasingly concentrated on drug offences'.[45] The reality is, drugs are a path to criminalisation for some people and a free pass for others.

The government's own evaluation of how effective their drug enforcement policies are, found limited evidence that stop and search even restricts drugs supply at all.[46] And regardless of large-scale drug seizures, the market for illicit substances remains resilient.[47] British people spend more on illicit drugs than they do in Aldi.[48] In 2016–2017, people in England and Wales spent more on drugs than they did at Boots or on EasyJet flights, a whopping £9.4 billion.[49]

Politicians' past drug use is so pervasive that Sky News has compiled a handy list of rumours and statements.[50] Of twenty-five European countries that submitted data on drug use, the UK had the highest number of cocaine users and the third highest for Ecstasy.[51]

Some of these people will be black. And although the British Crime Survey suggests that we use drugs at lower rates than white people, that can create a false discourse that *none of us* do.

In a review of Michaela Coel's hit BBC show *I May Destroy You*, writer Lakeisha Goedluck praises Cole's realistic depiction of young black women taking Class A drugs. She celebrates the complexity shown on screen, charting the highs and lows of drug taking, not solely good or evil but the shepherd of joy and danger. The two central characters, Arabella and Terry, are not drug dealers or addicts, they are 'black women navigating drugs and sex for their own gratification'.[52] I know these women exist, not just because I am one of them, but because I have met them at university and beyond.

There is a narrative I've seen posed online that drugs are

something that we just don't do in the black community, as if we're monolithic.[53] Admitting to having done them can also lead to criticism and backlash. I witnessed it unravel on Twitter shortly after the tragic death of Jamal Edwards, the music entrepreneur and founder of online platform SB.TV, at age thirty-one. When his mother, the singer and *Loose Women* panellist Brenda Edwards, shared that he died from arrhythmia after taking recreational drugs, some black people on Twitter claimed she shouldn't have revealed the cause of death, as if it invalidated his achievements.[54] Black people have to be perfect even in death.

Rather than pretending that drug taking is simply not happening, or that only bad people do it, what could we do to make it as safe as possible?

As part of a public policy module I took at the London School of Economics, we were given an exercise. We had to decide what the government's response should be to a new policy problem: the emergence of new psychoactive substances (aka legal highs or 'new' drugs that aren't yet controlled by the law). At first, I took an interest in the assignment for selfish reasons. I wanted to justify my drug taking. I had investigated the health risks before I'd gummed the MDMA crystals in 2011. But the exercise was important. It forced me to look outside of myself and consider how drug policy works in its own right and how controlling drugs impacts other people. I started to see it as a system that needed to change.

My partner for the project was a lovely, straight-laced, third-culture kid who was passionate about horses. She couldn't understand why anyone would voluntarily 'put random white powders up their nose' and I pretended to agree.

True policy nerds across the spectrum of political persuasions are united in their love of the evidence. Facts don't land in neutral space, they collect in a reservoir of our values and take their shape. But sometimes the data is so powerful that people with differing beliefs come to similar conclusions.

This was true for me and my uni buddy who at the time backed decriminalisation, whereby criminal penalties for the possession of drugs for personal use are removed, of which Portugal's drug strategy is the most famous example.

Since 2001, when decriminalisation and harm reduction policies were implemented, there's been a dramatic drop in drug-related deaths and crime, HIV and hepatitis infections, and incarceration rates.[55] Drug consumption hasn't increased and young people postpone experimentation with drugs until later in life.[56] 'Right wing parties opposing it said, oh, Portugal will become a paradise for drug users, our children will start using drugs in their milk bottles, the United Nations, they will punish you. Nowadays, there's a complete consensus around it. Everybody agrees that it was a good solution,' said Dr João Goulão, who designed the policy.

Decriminalisation has grown in popularity as a response to the failure of drug policy. The Royal College of Physicians, the Faculty of Public Health, the Royal Society for Public Health and British Medical Association all support it. Ghana, the Czech Republic, the Netherlands and Switzerland have also decriminalised all drugs, while thirty countries have some form of decriminalisation for some drugs.[57] Malta has become the first EU country to legalise the cultivation and consumption of cannabis for recreational use.[58] At the time of writing, the German chancellor Olaf Scholz of the Social Democrats is in talks with the Green party Free Democrats to legalise and regulate cannabis.[59] England even has some de facto decriminalisation, where individual chief constables have decided not to charge low-level drug users or to send them on education programmes instead.[60] And in January 2022, Sadiq Khan, the Mayor of London, said he may oversee trials led by the London Boroughs of Lewisham, Bexley and Greenwich to divert eighteen-to-twenty-four-year-olds found with small amounts of cannabis into drug courses or counselling instead of arresting them.[61]

Decriminalisation is a critical step. But it has less impact on the global illegal drug markets, how they operate and the people, mostly in developing countries but also in the UK, that are part of a violent supply chain. County lines, a particularly violent part of the UK drug supply chain, has gotten more media coverage and attention from MPs in recent years. I first came across it in a job interview for a children's charity in 2019. As part of the process, I had an hour to summarise a series of long policy documents on county lines and child exploitation. Since then, there have been numerous radio and TV documentaries, an investigation by the *Huffington Post*, and a dramatisation of the phenomenon in the popular Netflix show *Top Boy*.

County lines is a complex, cross-cutting issue that can involve: drugs, violence, gangs, safeguarding, modern slavery, missing people and the criminal and sexual exploitation of children, young people and vulnerable people.[62] It's a relatively new system of drug distribution that links coastal and rural areas, which have less of a police presence, to urban hubs. Young people are used as runners to transport money and drugs. The 'lines' refer to mobile phones that are used to control a young person who is delivering drugs, often to towns in a different county.

In 2018, around one in three people sentenced for supplying crack cocaine and one in four sentenced for supplying heroin were under twenty-one. It is a similar picture for the supply of cannabis.[63] The 'runners' are typically (but not exclusively) boys aged fourteen to seventeen, who are groomed with the promise of money, gifts and status, then deployed or coerced to carry out drug deals on a daily basis. Sexual and physical violence is commonly used as a form of control.[64]

Getting young people out of the drug trade is difficult. Knowing that the police target black youth, line runners started using more white young people who are not known to the authorities, whether that's social services or the police, so they are more likely to avoid detection. They use the police's racialised tactics, such as stop and search, against them.[65]

Former Metropolitan police constable Ali Hassan Ali told me that nearly everyone caught up in county lines is a victim. Talking about an older man who was running a drug line, he explained that in childhood, this man had witnessed domestic violence at home and not received love from his caregivers.

'[He] said to me, "I've never known what love is or empathy is. I don't know any of that." He just goes, "I could instantly kill someone and have no remorse." He looked me straight in the eye. He looked stone cold,' Ali said. This man believed he was giving the children on his line a better life, access to resources he himself was denied in childhood.

'He's basically groomed all these children to work on his line. He says, "I don't care anymore, and if anything, I'm giving them a better life because they're getting things that I never had." So he's looking at it in a very twisted sort of way where he thinks he's helping these kids by giving them money and a better lifestyle.'

During his keynote speech at the Conservative Party conference in 2019, Prime Minister Boris Johnson told the audience that the party was 'committing now to rolling up the evil county lines drugs gangs that prey on young kids and send them to die in the streets to feed the cocaine habits of the bourgeoisie.'[66] At first glance, that's an admirable aim. Similar sentiments have been shared by former Conservative Home Secretary Sajid Javid, the Labour Mayor of London Sadiq Khan and the former Metropolitan Police Commissioner Cressida Dick. It's true that powder cocaine use is linked to income, with most of the growth in the number of users over the past five years being driven by middle-class white men under thirty.[67]

But the substances that are the key drivers of 'county lines' are heroin and crack cocaine.[68] Most of the drug-related costs to individuals and society at large are concentrated here, with children and young people heavily involved in the trade. The use of these drugs is also strongly linked to deprivation and premature deaths.[69] The UK's powder cocaine market is associated with less violence. Although, this isn't permission to text your dealer for a gram – the international supply chain is extremely violent, bringing devastation to lives across Mexico and Colombia.[70] Even the domestic illicit weed industry in the UK has become a cesspit of modern slavery and violent cannabis farm wars between gangs wielding machetes.[71] It's just that a moral appeal to middle-class coke sniffers wouldn't necessarily bring an end to the county lines phenomenon in Britain and the severe violence it brings, even if that moral appeal was successful (which is debatable).

Shutting down county lines, and the illegal drug trade more broadly, requires a serious evaluation of which policies are working and which are making things worse. But when the government commissioned Dame Carol Black to lead part one of a review of drug policy in 2019, she was strictly forbidden from looking at whether our current drug laws actually work.[72] This is probably because a previous government evaluation of its own drug strategy had already found that it . . . doesn't work. It found drug policing is largely ineffective and that 'violence is an unintended consequence of enforcing drug laws'[73].

In a podcast for the charity the Children's Society, MP for the historic commuter town of Colchester, Will Quince, said that more MPs were raising the issue now it had spread outside of urban areas. 'We can't arrest our way out of this problem,' Quince told Scott Compton, then at the Children's Society. 'It's far deeper rooted than that.'[74]

The only way to wind down the black market for drugs is to legalise them. Colombia's Truth Commission report, published in 2022 to address the country's ongoing six-decade old conflict, concluded that without some form of legalisation of drugs, peace will not be achieved.[75] When I asked Adam Nicholls, the former Director of Transform Drug Policy, what he thought he framed it like this: 'You don't have pub landlords killing each other for market territory, right? Because you have a legal system and legal frameworks. You don't have that in the non-regulated system,' he said. 'You just have recourse to violence.'

• • •

The last time I saw my student drug dealer was in London in 2016. The UK was just about to vote (narrowly) to leave the European Union. He was dropping off four bags bulging not with MDMA or ketamine but with clothes and shoes. I had done a callout for donations for refugees on Facebook and he responded.

Their gang of four student dealers were sentenced to between eleven to fifteen years in 2018 for conspiracy to import, export and supply controlled drugs. Another student was convicted for assisting the offenders in packing the drugs for dispatch. The FBI shut down the dark web marketplace Silk Road in October 2013 and traced its server to Iceland. My uni dealer's details were found on there and the FBI tipped off the National Crime Agency (NCA) in Britain. They raided a flat in central Manchester where two of them lived, where they found thousands of pounds in cash, a baseball bat next to the front door and drugs including LSD, Ecstasy, ketamine and diazepam.[76] According to a report in *The Times*, prosecutors have so far been unable to trace their profits, which they claim are held in hidden accounts in bitcoin. The NCA investigators also told *The Times* how 'struck' they were by the middle-class background of all four members of the gang – two were even former pupils of Dr Challoner's Grammar School in Amersham, Buckinghamshire.* One investigator on the case said: 'They were from good backgrounds. As we dealt with them, during the interview process it was quite apparent we were dealing with highly intelligent individuals.'[77]

Sentencing the group to between seven and fifteen years, the judge, Michael Leeming, told Manchester Crown Court:

* Dr Challoner's Grammar School is a selective boys' grammar school in Buckinghamshire. According to the Good Schools Guide, it is often one of the top twenty state schools nationally with a reputation for academic excellence. https://www.goodschoolsguide.co.uk/schools/dr-challoners-grammar-school-amersham

> Drugs are a blight on our society. Misery and degradation is the typical result. As intelligent men, you will each appreciate the misery that is caused and contributed to by people like you. My duty is threefold: firstly, to protect the public from people like you. Second, to punish you, and third, to deter those who may be similarly minded to act this way in the future.[78]

I can only speak for myself here, but buying MDMA from these students did not bring me misery or degradation. Taking MDMA was joyous and getting it from them was safer than buying it off the street.[79] What did put me in danger was the lack of honest education about drugs and the risks involved in taking them. And it is the inebriation of the legal drug – alcohol – that has left me nearly drowning in danger time and time again, barely treading my way out of near misses. Unlike alcohol, Ecstasy didn't make me stumble onto the wrong train and wake up in Kent at 1 a.m. crying and clutching a Topshop bag or wake up in a hostel in Bangkok with few memories and US $80 mysteriously missing from my bag. It is alcohol that erased the final hour of my thirty-first birthday so that it lives not in my memories but in friends' retellings of it. It lives in the photos and fragmented flashbacks that I've stuck together into a facsimile of recollection.

That is not to minimise the harm illegal drugs – or any drug – can bring on individuals. I, for one, can't take MDMA often, because it can exacerbate anxiety and low moods (as can alcohol). I only know that because I admitted to taking MDMA to a therapist, who was able to advise me accordingly on how illicit drugs and alcohol might affect my mental health. And we must never devalue the seriousness of addiction, which is treated differently depending on your perceived class background. But as it stands, the system as it exists isn't keeping anyone safe. Whether it's the harm to users or the violence facing people caught up in county lines gangs or the criminal justice system: no one is winning. Adding these 4 people to the approximately 82,000 people who, on a given day, are in prison for drugs-related crime doesn't change that.[80]

Ultimately, all drugs – from alcohol to heroin – present risks to their users and the wider community. 'It's not that the drugs aren't dangerous and don't come with risks,' James Nicholls, the former director of Transform Drug Policy, told me. 'But those risks are amplified and exacerbated by prohibition.' Ideology has been trumping science for too long. It's time for public health experts to step in and design a new system.*

It won't be easy and there will be unintended consequences that we can't foresee. It requires UN treaties, protocols and conventions to be changed.** But we can't keep things as they are either. It is still very easy to get drugs and more people are dying as a result. Between 2010 and 2020, there was a 52 per cent increase in drug-related deaths – not a sign of policy success.[81] Drug use among eleven-to-fifteen-year olds increased by over 40 per cent between 2014 and 2019.[82]

'We'll just keep it as it is. That's not a neutral position,' Nicholls told me. 'That's defending the situation that has led to record numbers of drug-related deaths. It's led to massive disproportionality in policing. You can't just say, oh, well, I'll leave that for someone else.'

It's been over twenty years since the Misuse of Drugs Act was passed. It's failed. Ending drug prohibition sounds radical. In actuality, it's just sensible. It's facts over fictions and science over misplaced moralism.

'Do you know which drug gives you the longest sentence for dealing?' Professor David Nutt asks on the Novara Media podcast. '[It's] MDMA. Why is it MDMA? Because judges hate young people having fun.'[83]

---

* For more see research on drug harms see Nutt, D., *Drugs Without the Hot Air*, p.153.

** For more on the history of the UN protocols and the changes needed see Transform, *How to regulate stimulants*, p.192.

11 A guide to drug taking

'No business in the world is so dynamic, so restlessly innovative, so loyal to the pure free-market spirit as the global cocaine business,' wrote the author and journalist Roberto Saviano.[1] Because drugs are illegal they are unregulated, which means there are no rules in the traditional sense. When the treaties and laws are already being ignored and broken, a shadow set of protocols take their place. Even at its most basic, just picking up for a big night out with a few mates on the weekend comes with its own rules of engagement, a dialect of terms and phrases, and pretty impressive guerrilla marketing campaigns.

The number one rule: be middle class (and preferably white)

If you're middle class, you can pick up drugs without the fear of being arrested. Don't be scared – just make sure to not look poor and/or be a black male and you will be invisible to the police. It's always best to get a white person you know to pick up, if possible. And if you have future political aspirations, avoid any photographic evidence that's indisputable (action shots of you doing a key or obviously inflated pupils). If it's too late for that, just give the political version of a celebrity Notes app apology, with the lack of sincerity of a YouTuber doing an 'I'm so sorry' video after their racist tweets are exposed, to get you out of hot water:

'I was a bit wacky at university and smoked a joint or two. I did coke twice during my time working in banking/the media, but I regret it terribly and it really was only a few times and not endemic in the industry I worked in where everyone was at it at after-work drinks, the Christmas party and popular colleagues' birthdays. It was incredibly dangerous and stupid. I am, of course, a hypocrite, so I now back tough sentences for drug dealers because drugs are for criminals and none of this affects me personally anymore.'

How to find drugs

Drug dealing relies on a clandestine network of communication, tendrils of trust that support and sustain the entire operation. Like all the best restaurants, news of good-quality drugs spreads by word of mouth from friends and colleagues, has good service, and isn't so popular that it requires long periods of waiting before you can finally get your food.

Universities are awash with drugs, you can't swing a Fjällräven Kånken backpack without hitting a dealer. Numbers spread at the speed of STIs at an Athletics Union social. If you work in recruitment, advertising, finance, or for a media company, drugs will be pretty easy to find, just go to a few Friday night drinks and stay late enough for someone to bring out a baggie. Have no fear if you work for a charity, after a few drinks, hushed tones and allusions to electronic music or a recent trip to Berlin (or wherever the 'new Berlin' of that year is) you will know you've found your people. Look out for the person who slinks out of the pub for twenty minutes unexplained or the colleague who's always suggesting 'an afters' and ask for their drug dealer's number.

Direct marketing

Getting your product out there and setting it apart from the rest is vital to the success of any product and any business. Drug dealers can't take out billboards or do sponsored content, so they have to find other ways to get the message out. My favourite is still the Manchester dealers who put free samples of weed through the letterboxes of student houses – innovative and targeted. It beats the predictable whispers of *pills, coke, ket* in the smoking area.

Direct marketing via unsolicited messages is also a cornerstone of communication. Dealers share the same energy as market traders, with the approach of push notifications and pop-up ads. They're hard to ignore, brash and have a knack for flashing up on your home screen when you're at a family dinner with your phone turned face up. The tone is often hyper, as if to mimic the effect of the drugs on sale (well the uppers anyway).

ON FOR DELIVERIES TO GET YOUR FRIDAY NIGHT GOING. MANDY KET COKE EVERYTHING YOU NEED. SPECIAL OFFERS

If you're lucky, it will mostly be written in emojis, which keeps it fun and less obvious to the non-drug takers in your life. There are seasonal deals linked to the run-up to Christmas, New Year and even Valentine's Day-themed magic mushroom chocolates.

Glossary

❄️ Coke

💊 Ecstasy in pill or other form

🐴 🦄 Ketamine

😍🕺💃 MDMA

😴 😴 Valium

Good customer service

Good customer service is important. You can't send in a complaint to head office or Trading Standards if your drug dealer is a no-show. Being told 'I'm fifteen minutes away' every forty minutes over three hours is frustrating. If you're lucky, you might get a discount for the inconvenience. Note who has good customer service, stay loyal to them, and tell your friends – good service deserves a reward. When the Omicron variant of the Covid-19 virus swept through the UK in December 2021, my dealer offered letterbox deliveries for people self-isolating during the festive period. That is service.

Stay safe

If you're going to take drugs, take a harm reduction approach. Get your drugs tested, only take a small amount to start, avoid mixing different types of drugs (including alcohol) and take advice from professional sources like The Loop or Frank.[2]

12 But you have Beyoncé! On race and friendship

Friendship is the place in which a great majority of us have our first glimpse of redemptive love and caring community. Learning to love in friendships empowers us.[1]

bell hooks, *All About Love*

I don't know, maybe who you are now, and . . . who I am now just . . . don't fit any more.[2]

Molly Carter to her best friend Issa Dee, in *Lowkey Trying*, season four, episode nine of HBO's *Insecure*

On this day in 2016, I was the devil. I travelled on the Underground at rush hour with a set of flat-pack boxes. They're angular, designed for the vans and lorries that are their true destiny, not for 6 p.m. on a weekday in a crowded carriage. The cardboard pinched in the grip of my underarms, I was an unstable scarecrow. A woman from uni I hadn't seen in years spotted me from across the carriage. She was the only person to offer me a hand with the boxes. The rest of the passengers expressed mild contempt for the inconvenience.

Lucy had been working abroad and was only in London for a few days. Our chance encounter felt scripted. Here she was, on the same Tube, in the same carriage, at the same time as me, on the day I was struggling with all that cardboard. She asked me what the boxes were for and when I said I was moving flat, she asked me who I currently lived with and where I was moving to. When I said the name, she paused.

'I lived with her at uni. Get out. Don't feel guilty,' she told me. 'You know when her boyfriend broke up with her, she made a fake Facebook account and started sending him racist messages?' she added. Then she shared some further details I won't repeat. As the doors opened at her stop she encouraged me to move on with my life and not look back.

It felt like the permission I needed. The permission I had been seeking to end the friendship for months.

Sonia was the beautiful blonde who had claimed at a party that the reason her female friendships broke down repeatedly was due to jealousy. Every year or two she would cycle through a new friendship group with a stunning regularity. She would fall out with them, brand them 'toxic' bullies, then insert herself into a new group while positioning herself as a victim. I had lived with Sonia for close to a year and the tenancy was coming to an end.

Our friendship had started to disintegrate when I got onto a traineeship programme. I wanted to work in public policy for a charity. I had sent out over one hundred applications in just over a year with little success. Most people I knew from school and uni were in a similar position. We found solace in the knowledge that we were all going through the same thing. The fact that within a year or two, the bulk of us had gotten an entry-level spot in our hypercompetitive and desirable industries says a lot. The contraction of the graduate job market was by no means imagined, but our debilitating feelings of failure and precarity were probably exaggerated. Nevertheless, when we started looking for work in 2014, the market hadn't recovered from the 2008 financial crisis. So we spent 50–60 per cent of our salaries on rent and the rest on cheap food, crop tops and nights out, making the most of not having responsibility for anything other than ourselves.

The day I got the policy job, Sonia got fired from her internship. Financially, I knew she would be covered until she found something else.

The scales of our friendship were already tipping towards imbalance when fewer people had come to her birthday than mine. The job added too much weight. It was the critical Jenga piece that when pulled brought the whole structure to the ground. I started the job in mid-August and by early September the friendship was a wreck, fractured and dysfunctional.

We had an Indian summer in 2015 so the sunshine leaked through into September. I was standing with Sonia and another woman, let's call her Melissa. At an intersection with Brixton Station Road, surrounded by the markers of burgeoning gentrification, Sonia accused me of not being supportive enough of her efforts to find a new job. Melissa had been helping her with her CV and job applications but I had not. Then she started shouting at me in the street.

'It's not fair. You have perfect friends and a perfect mum and a perfect life,' she told me. 'Now you've got your new job. Just perfect perfect PERFECT. You're not being supportive and you have a chip on your shoulder because you were born on a council estate.'

I started crying.

I apologised to Sonia for not supporting her job search. Getting fired from a job is upsetting. It felt plausible that I'd gotten caught up in my new job – the need to make a good impression and the excitement of new colleagues. After the public reckoning, we went out to my friend's birthday in Hackney Wick and all was forgiven. But I couldn't sleep that night. Her words, her screaming at me, tossed and turned as I did, unable to sleep deeply.

I wasn't living my life to spite Sonia, although she described it as if I were. With hindsight, I see an implicit subtext in her words. The job and the friends and my relationship with my mum were the tenets of the kind of life she had been promised and felt she deserved. Yet here I was, living it when, relative to her, I was meant to be subordinate. Or at the very least a side character.

The next day, I told her that the way she spoke to me and what she had said wasn't appropriate. The next five months were hell.

If a boyfriend had shouted at me in the street for the offence of not helping him with his CV, I would have been told he needed to go to therapy. Someone may have even noted the term 'chip on your shoulder' as particularly out of line. If he then refused to go to therapy and continued to lash out, I would have been told that you can only help people who are ready and willing to accept it. Instead, I was told I needed to 'support Sonia' by multiple mutual friends to the detriment of my own mental health. Even when she had tried to lump me with her portion of the bills as punishment for moving out of the house and sent a mutual friend a long Facebook rant about me, someone still had the audacity to ask me to reach out to her because they were worried she might be caught up in a pyramid scheme. While lifestyle influencers will implore women to stop trying to 'fix' heterosexual men, I was asked if I felt like I had 'failed' because I wasn't able to help Sonia.

'Friendship is the most free-choice relationship. It's a relationship that is mutual, reciprocal . . . it has something that demands equity,' the psychotherapist Esther Perel said on her podcast, *Where Should We Begin?*[3] You are not obligated to be friends with anyone in the way that biological family often demands. Women are, however, made to feel obligated to support people even if it's bad for them. And black women are expected to carry everyone.

• • •

I am fortunate that most of my close formative friendships were healthy and positive. Driving past a road that leads to one of my friends' parents' houses can drench me in a jarring yet comforting nostalgia. I get flashes of names carved into desks in the biology lab (*Val & Kim 4eva*), gossip shared in the back of my notebook

(I saw so and so with such and such in town leaving the cinema – together!), languid summers in other people's gardens and driving in convoy to West Wittering beach. Three of us passed out on the pull-out in my front room after a night out in town. Mum making us bacon sandwiches and letting us shower during Reading Festival.

Lots of them are still mainstays, a thread to my past selves. Other friends have come later through university to the workplace and house shares and even friends' workplaces and house shares. You are by their side for funerals, they send you flowers when you are down. All relationships are ultimately about what we owe to each, the unsaid yet mutually agreed ways we should behave. Except that mutual agreement can be illusory, implicit and assumed. I know what I expect from a friendship and I assume that we're on the same page about things. But anything based on an assumption is ripe for misunderstanding and conflict.

Which means that every day we harm people, whether we mean to or not. I know I have. That's why I've changed all my friends' (and enemies') names throughout this book. I erase their names from the story, as if I've soused them in that smelly fluid from those nineties double-ended pens, until their names disappear and I can write the story again without them in it. I say this because, like the philosopher Kwame Anthony Appiah wrote in his *New York Times Magazine* column on ethics, I believe that 'friendship can and should err on the side of tolerance, but big-enough vices – beams rather than motes – can be an obstacle to it'.[4] At what point then, should tolerance stop and boundaries begin?

• • •

Even at age seven, I somehow picked out people with similar values for friendship. It wasn't true of everyone I hung out with, more an overarching trend. Now grown-up, there are a disproportionate number of us working for charities, public services or in the arts. We're not chiefly driven by money. I didn't actively seek any of that out as a child or teenager. I ended school wanting to be both a public servant and to marry a millionaire. It's just that like any relationship, friendships grow together or apart. And I don't think it's an accident that the people I still spend time with from my early years, although they are very different people, have overlapping ideas about what matters in life. It's easy to base friendships on shared interests in music genres and mutual appreciation of *High School Musical* when you're sixteen. It can't sustain you into adulthood, with all the challenges and self-realisation that can bring.

As we get older, our understanding of ourselves changes. Our identities aren't static, but constantly evolving. We carve them out of the materials we are given, the life events that shape us and the public attitudes that alter perceptions of us, whether we feel they represent us or not. What we do with all that is up to us but there are patterns in how people respond from childhood, through adolescence and into adulthood to the world around them.

'As one's awareness of the daily challenges of living in a racist society increases, it is immensely beneficial to be able to share one's experiences with others who have lived them,' US psychologist and academic Dr Beverly Daniel Tatum writes in her book, *Why Are All the Black Kids Sitting Together in the Cafeteria?* 'Even when white friends are willing and able to listen and bear witness to one's struggles, they cannot really share the experience.'[5]

With age, it is obvious to me why my mum sent me to an African-Caribbean after-school club and Saturday School, and encouraged me to build friendships there. Racism, like death and taxes, is one of life's certainties, but as a child I only had vague conceptions of them, until unannounced they appeared and affected me directly. My life would have been much lonelier and disorienting if Mum hadn't had the foresight to send me there.

'The friends that I have now, we've known each other since

[age] fifteen, sixteen,' a friend told me. 'What's funny is, one of them really spawned from the fact that we were looking at each other like, oh, shit, we're the only black guys here! How you doing, man? And it's literally been since day. He's my best friend.'

For ethnic minorities in their teenage years and young adulthood, it's common for their racial awareness to grow as they do.[6] It can be the cumulative effect of a lot of little incidents, pinpricks of injustice that sting on impact and eventually leave a bruise; say, an old white woman reporting my car as abandoned to the police and putting a sign on the windscreen. Or a highly publicised tragedy like the murder of Stephen Lawrence or George Floyd can bring it to the fore. Once you see it, you can't unsee it.

Dr Tracey Reynolds interviewed young black people of Caribbean heritage from Birmingham, London, Manchester and Nottingham and found similar patterns of developing a racial identity through adolescence. Her study also revealed something else, that the young black people who moved from predominantly white primary schools to predominantly white secondary schools in affluent areas had a more ethnically mixed group of friends. Because of that, they developed their racial consciousness later in life or at home through their immediate and extended family.[7]

Although this process of figuring out your identity won't ring true for everyone, it reflects my own journey. I got most of my cultural reinforcement at home and with family: the food, the music and the conversations on race, which were absent socially. But it was at university that it really took off, aided in part by the opportunity to study history that countered what the academic Patricia Hill Collins called *controlling images*, media depictions or even curricula designed to make racism, sexism, poverty, and other forms of social injustice appear to be either non-existent or natural and normal.[8] There are university modules I took that helped me to narrate the story of my life, from Saint Ann, Jamaica, to east Reading, and the joy and love and rejection and violence that brought me into being. There is a consequence to this process, though. Now you have the words to describe who you are accurately, is everyone ready to hear them?

• • •

'I would get to the point where I'm losing friends, because I have to respect myself,' my friend Roy said. 'I don't accept that in any way, shape or form, I don't do those jokes.' Roy initially grew up in a working-class area, a mixed community where black and white working-class people grew up together. There, an unspoken understanding of what was acceptable existed. There was a mutual respect. Everyone knew racist language was unacceptable and not to cross the line. Then, he moved to a middle-class area and found this respect lacking. 'It wasn't even as if they were going around saying the n-word or whatever. But it was when people flirt on that borderline, and it's, it's kind of meant to be "banter". I just – I have never accepted it.' He felt the other black guys in the group had a higher tolerance for this behaviour, or at least dealt with it differently. As they got older, this has changed.

I'm still friends with a lot of people from school, uni and work. I'm not friends with all of them, though. There are the people I've simply lost touch with as you build your lives in separate cities. I occasionally like their Instagram posts, perhaps an image of their wedding or baby or a nice snap of them with their parents. There are the friends I rarely see but when I do we smoothly slot into the groove of familiarity. There are a few who I think I'd get on really well with but know I'm unlikely to ever meet up with. Friendships from work can fade when everyone has moved on to a new organisation, pulling the anchor out from under you and casting you all adrift. But there are others, too, who I'm glad are no longer in my life. There are also the people I actively dislike, whose 'jokes' aren't banter but are racist and homophobic, and I loathe that once a year I have to interact with them at so-and-so's birthday.

As part of the research project 'Where friends are made. Contexts, Contacts, Consequences', Utrecht University sociologist Gerald Mollenhorst studied 1,007 men and women in the Netherlands between the ages of eighteen and sixty-five; reinterviewing 604 of them seven years later. He differentiated between two types of friend: confidants who you would go to if you wanted to talk about serious personal issues, and acquaintances, like a neighbour you might ask to borrow a hammer from. He found that in the seven-year gap, the interviewees had replaced nearly half of their friendship group. Only 30 per cent of the friends mentioned seven years prior still made the cut when he reinterviewed them.[9] Why do some of these old friendships fizzle out while others stay afloat?

In 2021, Mollenhorst and his colleagues published some follow-up work that looked at the role difference plays in relationship ties unravelling. People tend to have a preference for people who are similar to them from the moment they decide who to walk up to at a party and strike up some small talk with, who from work they invite to their birthday, and who to ask for advice. Conversations are smoother and you're more likely to have similar interests and share hobbies. And if someone has gone through similar experiences to you, they can offer support and advice that makes you feel seen and understood.

Mollenhorst discovered that friends of different genders, ages and ethnicities were more likely to be lost over time than people from the same background. People moving away to live in a new town, city or country also made it more likely the friendship would end. This makes sense, think of a friend you worked with who changes jobs or a friend who moves out of the city and has a baby. It's harder to meet up for a spontaneous coffee, go for drinks or to carve out time for deep, meaningful chats than before. Time, however, is a protective factor. The longer you've been friends, the more likely it is you'll stay friends. After twenty years, the differences between us and our friends have little impact on the chance we'll stay pals. The only exception is a difference in ethnicity. The likelihood the friendship between people of different ethnicities will break down or phase out is profoundly higher, even after fifty years. [10]

Why this happens is unclear and isn't explored in the paper. But some of the key researchers in the field of friendship and social networks claim that the principle of equality is key to maintaining successful friendship networks. Friends with big social differences between them tend to be harder to keep alive.[11]

In another research paper on friendship, this time based in the US, two findings struck me. One was that women tended to have deeper friendships, both across racial boundaries and more generally, because they shared more of their thoughts and feelings with each other. Patriarchy is a prison for men too, and the lack of emotional openness associated with 'traditional' masculinity can be a barrier to building bonds. Roy and his friends are working to challenge that. 'My friends have now also got therapists. It's really just cool that we can just sit down and just talk. As young black men it's quite nice that we can just sit around and say, hey look, this is how it made me feel,' he told me. 'I think as, as men, we have these automatic boundaries, if you hit me, then I'm going to fight. Or if you say something to my mother. Out of fear of feeling vulnerable.'

The second key finding from the research paper was that participants said they avoided talking about racially charged events like police brutality against black men, for fear of destroying friendships with people of a different ethnicity or being misunderstood.[12]

• • •

'I hate to say it but I think it's true that there is a hierarchy of who gets to feel what and when and I don't think my feelings are valued or acknowledged in the same level in which a white woman's feelings are acknowledged or valued,' Antoinette, a thirty-five-year-old black woman from Dallas, told the hosts of the NPR podcast *Code Switch*.

She was explaining an interaction she'd had with a white friend and colleague, who was upset by the blunt tone of a text message she'd sent. Antoinette's ceiling had started leaking that day, so she was busy coordinating the maintenance staff who came to fix it. She was trying to clean up the floor and also look after her child. Even though she didn't feel like her friend was being fair or taking into account her situation, she apologised anyway. 'I'm leading with someone else's feelings and emotions before my own,' she said.[13]

The person whose feelings take priority, and even whose life events are more important, has, until recently, rarely been me. It's showed itself when, over lunch, I announced a job and instead of congratulations, I was told: 'Oh our friend so-and-so would be good at that.' At the pre-drinks and that awful birthday lunch when I had to sit and make small talk with that peripheral acquaintance who multiple people had told me is racist. No one asked how I felt before or after. It's just assumed you'll do it. I never felt it more than when I was out every night drinking just to avoid having to go to my hideous house share with Sonia, and so many mutuals spurred me to keep going, at the expense of myself. Friendship is powerful but if it feels like an unbalanced, self-sacrificial project, it might be time for it to end.

There is a difference between being kind and being nice. I'm a kind person, but I have stopped being nice. Kind is thoughtful birthday presents and crossing town to support your friend when they are low. Sometimes setting boundaries is the kindest thing you can do for yourself and the people you're erecting them around. Caring for someone can mean walking away, not unquestioning loyalty. Being nice is fake. It's pretending you don't mind when you're hurting. Being nice is holding your breath and leaving an airless silence that 'keeps the peace', when you want to scream. It serves no one, least of all, you.

In our early twenties, Dora and I would frequent parties and get into heated political conversations with libertarians and rich white guys with dubiously sourced inheritances. After a drink or two, we got a thrill out of telling them exactly what we thought and I would hazard a guess that they enjoyed it too. So we relished the conflict. But Dora and I are politics freaks and I am aware that this is not most people's idea of a good time. Arguing on Facebook on a Friday night with someone claiming market forces alone could have ended apartheid in South Africa? Sign me up. There were no stakes really in any of these conversations, nothing to lose. It wasn't dinner with your best friend's family, it was just a party.

It's common, especially in Britain where we're obsessed with civility and respectability, to avoid conflict and challenging conversations to 'keep the peace', to not 'ruin' an event by making people feel discomfort or to accommodate other people's needs before our own, whether the audience are your best friends or complete strangers.

Sometimes this can be the right thing to do. I'm unlikely to cause a scene at someone's wedding. Sometimes I just can't be arsed, like when a random guy on acid started telling me, unprompted, about his Nigerian friend when I am not Nigerian, then asked for my take on racism in football (I swiftly moved to another part of the party). But conflict in the right context can lead to healthier relationships that come from a place of honesty and vulnerability.

Things came to a head for Roy and his friendship group in their group chat. It had been years in the making. 'One of the boys said something in a group. And it was like, well, here we are, we're gonna address these things now,' he told me. Some of the people in the group chat run a club night and the next one was booked for a venue in Tottenham, North London. A white member of the group posted something along the lines of: 'I would go but, you know, it's in Tottenham and you know, I don't want to get stabbed or something like that,' Roy told me. 'Jordan was, like, are you fucking joking? This is our event. You're my friends. Like, what the fuck is wrong with you? And I think that sparked just a whole lot of well – to be honest with you this is not the first time. I think it was healthy.'

I once forgave a white woman who made me cry with her derogatory comment about black men as partners, even though she never apologised (she hadn't even dated any black men). I no longer have any interest in this silence, staying quiet, internalising discomfort or letting things go so that everyone else can have a good time or to keep a friendship intact or in a desperate bid to avoid the 'angry black girl' or 'overly emotional woman' trope. Now, I have boundaries.

There is a lot to be said for working on childhood friendships and having people in your life with different political beliefs, interests and life experiences. But I don't think a relationship is really serving me if it's built on the suppression of my true feelings and fundamental principles. And how do we decide, in any given situation, whose needs should matter more?

I asked Roy how the other white people in the group chat responded. 'There's one or two of them that just don't like confrontation anyway, so it's very much, you know, very vanilla responses,' he said. 'But I think there were definitely lessons learned in terms of, like, this is not going to run any more. So I think it was really, it was a really good moment.'

'To converse is to risk the unravelling of the said and the unsaid. To converse is to risk the performance of what's held by the silence,' the acclaimed author and academic Claudia Rankine wrote in her book *Just Us*. Her book is essentially a documentation of her conversations with white people, both friends and strangers, and what that tells us about white identity in America.

In one of her essays, 'Social contract', a white woman at a dinner party disrupts a discussion about the role racism played in Donald Trump's election by cooing over a plate of homemade brownies that have just arrived for dessert. The social cue had been cast and the conversation cut off and redirected. Rankine refuses to stay silent, breaking the unspoken rules of engagement. She knows she will never be invited to this dinner party again.[14]

The Brexit referendum sparked concern about how divided Britain has become. Those deeply embedded generational and political fault lines had been there for a while, it's only that the ground shifted and exposed them. How we try to build bridges over these canyons of disagreement is an important question. In the quest for that though, we've conflated two different ideas: the lack of space for good-faith dialogue, particularly online, and having red lines on serious political issues, particularly ones that directly affect you.

Research by Ipsos Mori and the Policy Institute at King's College London looked into political differences that divide British society and whether people are willing to be friends 'across the line'. Nearly 60 per cent of the people they surveyed say they support the Black Lives Matter (BLM) movement. People who opposed the BLM movement are more likely to be over fifty and are much more likely to vote for the Conservative Party.

BLM supporters are twice as likely as BLM opponents to say, 'It's difficult to be friends with someone from the other side.' The researchers framed it as if this made BLM supporters less open-minded. I find this line of thought ridiculous.

If you do not support the BLM movement – we're obviously not friends. When I scroll through my timeline, and suddenly without my consent, my vision is assaulted with moving images of a black man being killed by the police, nestled between edgy shitposts and cat memes, that is more than a political disagreement to me, it is life and death. This is a justice issue, not a debate at the Oxford Union. And while I might have to work with you or tolerate you, I do not owe you friendship. We conflate too readily differences in political opinion with dehumanising beliefs.

I try to make space for ideas that I disagree with and the people who hold them. I struggle to do that for what I see as wilful ignorance or delusion. What is interesting about the study by King's College London is that they also tracked people's views on BLM with their beliefs about measurable facts about race. They found that 77 per cent of BLM supporters correctly identified that black African, Caribbean or Black British employees earned around 9 per cent less than their white counterparts in 2018. BLM opponents were almost half as likely to think this is the case, with 39 per cent believing it's true.[15] I'm not looking for cookie cut-outs of myself to share my dreams and anxieties with in a pub garden. I do yearn to be living in the same reality as them though, and if they are living in an imagined version of England that I know to be false, that's a canyon I'm not willing to traverse.

I do try to err on the side of tolerance. A conversation with stakes comes with risks, including the risk of hurting people and misunderstandings. People use the wrong words sometimes. They change their minds when they get new information. There's nothing wrong with that.

I have a friend of decades' long who ended an argument about cultural appropriation with the phrase 'But you have Beyoncé!' I put cultural appropriation in the 'irritating but there are bigger fish to fry' category. It's a symptom of racial inequality, not a cause. When I see the Kardashians being Kardashians or white faux hippies with dreads in Bristol using 'counterculture' as rebellion or to seem vaguely interesting, I file it in the 'That's Annoying' folder and carry on with my day. Black people facing school exclusion or being refused job interviews because of their afro-textured hair does piss me off though.* It's a double standard and no amount of Beyoncé is going to make it better. This was my mid-twenties and I had stopped letting things go. I didn't invite said friend to my birthday party and she bought me an apology plant. 'I saw it as an argument to win, not as something deeper,' she said. We're still friends and the plant still lives.

---

* For more see the Halo Collective campaign, https://halocollective.co.uk/

When George Floyd was murdered, I received many well-meaning messages from white people 'checking-in'. My home screen clogged with notifications, a downpour of messages flooding my inbox. He was still dead. Racism still existed. The anxiety of Covid-19 continued to infect my dreams. Now I had to think of something to say to all of these white people. Burdensome life admin. The phenomenon was so common the *New Yorker* satirised it with a cartoon and a black man had to write a *New York Times* op-ed telling white people to stop it. That's what I get for all those years in private school. If I had received no messages, I would have also been furious. Or as the journalist Yomi Adegoke said in *British Vogue*: 'I'm angry that so many are preoccupied with appearing to do something, and then angry at the white people who say nothing. I'm angry in every direction, and realise that this may be a case of white people being damned if they do and damned if they don't. But I can't say it feels particularly unjust, when black people are being killed simply for being black.'[16]

I didn't know what I wanted white friends to do. With space, I know now what I wish white friends had done instead of sending me a message at the behest of a viral Instagram slideshow. It's to stop prioritising keeping the peace, whether I'm in the room or not. There is a time and a place, of course. You don't have to make things awkward at Grandma's eightieth. You also don't have to tell me the racist thing your gran said at her eightieth without cause.

In the *Here to Slay* podcast, writer and academic Tressie McMillan Cottom and writer and activist Roxane Gay interview Claudia Rankine. She tells them that some white people think being able to talk about racism accurately and sensitively with people of colour is the end, rather than the beginning. 'What we actually need is for them to graduate to the next level – being able to have those conversations with white family and friends,' she says. 'That's the political project.'[17]

• • •

I now think differently about friendship and what I want from it. I now know that you don't have to keep someone in your life who makes you feel consistently awful, just because they are in pain. I have red lines that trace the outer limits of what I can welcome into my life, whether that's behaviour or beliefs and the values that scaffold them. Life is too short to pretend that you care for people you don't. So I want to spend it with people who want the world to be better for others, not just themselves, even if they're not sure how to make that happen. I allow friendships to drift as life's prevailing winds blow us in different directions but try hard to distinguish them from the types of bonds that just need a little bit more care. I want friends who can tell me when I'm wrong but stop short of judgement.

I've accepted that my personal relationships don't have to be activism. I'm not required to make my friendships with white people a racial justice advocacy project. There is a lot of work to be done on racism but this isn't the work required. I don't mean this in the sense of the 'Google is your friend' rhetoric that implores people to do their own research. Lots of us may loathe the idea of explaining how racism operates and what anti-racism looks like in our day-to-day lives when we want some space for a soft life. But people are not born with all the knowledge and, even if it's tedious, educating white people is a necessary part of building the racial justice movement. But people have to meet you halfway. You can bring a white friend an 'anti-racist' reading list but you can't make them read it. And you don't have to stick around if they don't.

Because life keeps getting harder. Parents start dying. Jobs are lost and careers you once loved start to curdle. Romantic relationships end as the heat and pressure of life morphs people into new shapes that don't slot together neatly like they used to. All I want now are people who show up as best they can and I'll try too, so we can muddle through the ecstasy, mundanity and devastation of it all together.

13 How to find a flatmate

Durham Uni hunz group chat*
*fictional but inspired by true events

24 June

Hattie
Hi babes! Celia and Paul are moving out and going to Thailand for a year ☹. Got to find a new flat 😩.

Cressida
Nooooooooooo. Omg. What are you gonna do?

Missy
Soooo sad. Can you stay with your sister and dishy dave in Clapham until you find a place? Stressful.

Hattie
Don't call him dishy dave! Yeah I'm gonna head there for a bit next month. I don't want to live with randoms again erghhh.

Missy
I know. The worst. I'm sure you'll find somewhere.

5 July

Cressida
How's the search going?

Hattie
Just finished my Spareroom ad. What do you think? http://spareroom.co.uk/basicbitchadvert0218

Ad ref #0218
26 YEAR OLD YOUNG PROFESSIONAL CREATIVE LOOKING FOR DOUBLE ROOM

Hi!
I'm Hattie. I'm 26 and my lovely flatmates Celia and Paul are abandoning me for a year and off to Thailand ☹. I'm looking for a nice flat share with a group of young professional women. I work in a creative agency in Old Street as a creative and love to go out for drinks on the weekend and stay in and watch a bit of Love Island in the week with some wine ☺. Quite big on CrossFit and cycling (looking preferably for a place with some bike storage). I'm a clean, tidy and respectful gal but not anal about it! I love going out and having fun but also can't say no to a night in and a Deliveroo. Oh and I come with a Barbican membership! Like to have fun but my job can get quite intense so not on weekdays! Volunteer on Thursdays. Looking for somewhere close to Brixton – 5–10 minute walk from the station.

Cressida
Love it! Maybe add brunch as well?

Hattie
Good shout!

Missy
God it's worse than writing a Hinge profile.

Cressida
Lol! So true. They're always like 'love to stay in but also to go out. I love a roast on a Sunday. I love the canal.' We get it. We all like a roast. We all love the canal.

Hattie
Is my ad basic?

Missy
No babe!

Cressida
No! It's great!

Missy
How's your sis?

Hattie
Dishy Dave proposed!! Really need to move out.

8 July

Hattie
Is Peckham dangerous? Mum's been watching a Panorama and is worried about gangs.

Cressida
You know I only do West.

Missy
No!! Peckham's cool now. Lots of hot guys and the back bit's got great restaurants now. Jay Rayner wrote about one of them and now it's impossible to get a table . . . Have you watched that film Blue Story?

Hattie
Nope. What's it about?

Missy
Don't watch it babe.

<u>12 July</u>

Cressida
How's the flat hunt?

Hattie
Saw this amazing place with a garden. And close to the park but they chose someone else. Feeling rejected ☹.

Cressida
Oh nooo. You'll find somewhere.

Hattie
I think I spoke too much about Celia and Paul. I was like oh they're my best friends from uni and I'm going to miss them so much and they always take care of the plants. Scared I'm gonna kill all the plants hahaha. Think it put them off. Like talking about an ex on the first date. Plus they have loads of plants. Plantmageddon.

Cressida
Boo.

Missy
Told you it's worse than dating.

Cressida
Remember when you lived with Carol @Missy? She just hid from you guys all year and then moved out in the middle of the night?

Missy
Can't forget. My worst ex.

Cressida
@Hattie would you live with a couple and just you?

Hattie
No way. Celia and Paul were an exception.

Cressida
Not even me and Luke?

Hattie
Especially not you and Luke. You're the worst.

Cressida

Hattie
I'm joking!

Missy
I don't want to live with any couples. It's better if they live somewhere else so you can get the flat to yourself half the week. Otherwise they're just there all the time taking up the sofa.

18 July

Hattie
Hey babes. Just been to see this flat. Looks cute and two flatmates seem nice. Got a garden and big double room. A PR and a freelancer. Only £750 a month.

Missy
Amazing! Are you gonna go for it?

Cressida
Bills or without bills?

Hattie
Without bills

Not sure.

Missy
How come?

Hattie
They're a bit . . . intense. Like they have a Black Lives Matter sign in the window. Obvs I support #BLM but it might be a bit much?

Cressida
It's a bit much. Unless they're black? Then it's probably ok.

Hattie
One of them is. Christina.

Cressida
Yeah then its fine I think.

Wednesday

Hattie
Hey babes. Heather and Chrissy got me that book, *Why I'm No Longer Talking to White People About Race* for Christmas. Is that passive aggressive? Thinking about moving out. Feeling ganged up on.

14 Atheism? Faith in the black community

Mum let me stop going to Sunday School when I was quite young, after asking me if I enjoyed it and me telling her that I didn't really. She remembered how boring she herself had found it as a child. So my only lasting memories of Sunday School are the suitably dramatic. The image of me throwing a glass of squash over a boy who had said something mean to me lives on. I had seen someone do the same thing on *EastEnders* in the Old Vic pub so it felt like an appropriate response. Although the memory is an old, overexposed photograph that's worn around the edges. The faces are blurry and faded but the action and characters are still just about visible. It was one of those moments where you sense that a grown-up is telling you off but also finds what you've done incredibly funny and is trying to stifle a smirk. The other was getting a comic strip explaining the evils of Halloween. The cartoon sketches of hellish fires had a visceral impact until I eventually celebrated the pagan holiday in lower-sixth, age seventeen. I still believed in God but figured He had bigger things to worry about than a teenager with a Topshop angel halo on her head dancing to pop music in a community theatre hall.

Earlier that year, when I had non-pulmonary tuberculosis, I lay in the hospital bed and did something that, at the time, was relatively routine – I prayed. I didn't know what was wrong with me yet, only that a sabre of a needle was stuck in my side, the economy was going south, and so was my health and I was scared. As a child and tween, I was violently happy, so much so that I was described in our prep school Leavers' Book as: 'Fun, smiley and never sad (well not usually anyway).' My rippling currents of insecurities were mild, never really strong enough to destabilise me emotionally. I'd faced some adversity but never too much. Although I didn't have everything that I wanted (I hadn't had sex of any kind. I'd never been clubbing and under-eighteens night didn't count), everything had more or less kept to the script and any revisions or edits had simply made the story better than I had previously imagined it could be. It was all going according to plan – God's plan for me.

My mid-to-late teens also felt like purgatory. I was in the Waiting Room of my Real Life, soon to be called up for my long-awaited appointment with adulthood: the parties, the sexcapades*, the travels that would all be mine. I constructed elaborate fantasies of the future, where I was ambiguously successful, rich, and pursued by glamorous and desirable men while also maintaining a purpose-driven career that 'helped' people in an ill-defined way. I could live in these delusions for hours (probably the after-effect of being an only child for so long and living in my head). I'd only broken a handful of rules and not collected the most important experience of all: romantic love.

I hadn't lived the way I wanted to yet. I was desperate and so I prayed desperately. I begged God to keep me alive and promised that if He did, I would live my life in a new way. I would prioritise happiness, stockpile experiences with the hunger and strategy we'd once used to collect Pokémon cards, take risks even if they scared me. And I would go to church more because I rarely did.

If you have read this book in order you'll know I kept up one side of the bargain.

• • •

* Sexual escapades and general drama.

A few days after the general election in December 2019, an acquaintance got in touch to gauge my interest in a job with a newly elected MP. I managed to call back a few days later, on a Sunday, sitting at my kitchen table.

'You're not at church then?' he asked me, surprised. I don't know if he'd already been that day or had skipped that particular Sunday. But I knew he was a believer.

'I've not been to church in years. I can't remember the last time I went that wasn't a wedding,' I told him.

'Weird . . . OK anyway . . .' he said, moving on to the topic at hand.

That might seem rude but he was right in a sense – being black and not being religious is not the norm in Britain. If being a weirdo is not conforming to what's expected, then strange is what I am.

The British Social Attitudes survey found that one in four members of the public stated, 'I do not believe in God,' with younger people less likely than their parents to have any religious belief.[1] But in the 2011 Census (which has ethnic breakdowns of the data), 69 per cent of black groups identify as Christian and 15 per cent as Muslim – over 85 per cent have a religious belief. Only 7 per cent of black people in Britain ticked 'no religion'. In contrast, 27 per cent of white British people selected 'no religion'.[2]

At the time of writing, the most recent Census has dropped but so far, they have only evaluated the top level data. I don't know what the new figures for ethnic minorities will tell us. For the overall population though, the 2021 Census is the first time that less than half of the population of England and Wales described themselves as "Christian". And this time round, more people ticked "no religion", increasing from 25 per cent of people in 2011 to 37 per cent in 2021.[3]

Identifying with a religion and actively embodying it through your actions are not the same thing. There are levels of engagement with faith that descriptive statistics like this can hide. In a YouGov survey commissioned by Humanists UK, they asked if people not only identified with a religion, but also what that meant for them. Only a third said they ticked the 'Christian' box because they 'believe in the teachings of Christianity'. Nearly 60 per cent said it was because they had been christened and nearly 50 per cent because they were brought up to think of themselves as Christian (you could tick more than one box).[4] This sits alongside declining church attendance and ageing congregations. In 2019, the Sunday attendance at Church of England services averaged at 690,000 adults, fewer than 1 per cent of the population. A third of those attending church were aged seventy or over.[5]

But the limited data I could find on black people and faith tells a different story. In the Ethnic Minority British Electoral Surveys, 72 per cent of black Caribbean and 92 per cent of black African respondents said religion was 'very' or 'extremely' important to them. Over 80 per cent of both groups followed religious practices such as praying. Almost all the black Caribbean people who took part said they were Christian, although they were the minority group least likely to go to their place of worship regularly.[6] The number of church members have been kept stable by migration and the rise in Evangelical and Pentecostal venues that tend to have black-majority congregations.[7] And while few millennials attend church regularly (I couldn't find anything conclusive on Gen Z), it's immigrants and their descendants who are going.[8]

But when I'm sitting at a wedding or funeral, I do not identify with what is being said. I see beauty in it: in the ritual, in the celebration of life and death, in the certainty and order. I'm calmed by the routine, reassured by the promise of better days, and am in awe of the sentence structure of the verses and the soul of gospel songs. I lower my eyes and try to bring my desires to life. I hear the sermon's lyricism and it gives meaning to the random arcs and bends of my days and any discomfort that accompanied them. But I know I don't believe what I'm hearing.

Questioning faith was slow and gradual. There was no epiphanic moment of clarity or definitive event. In our GCSE beliefs and values class (aka religious studies), we learnt about St Thomas Aquinas and the first cause argument, that the world that man observes must have been brought into being by God as the first cause, everything else following it.[9] A classmate told me she didn't find it very convincing. The tight stitches of religion loosened slowly and I wore faith lightly, something I lived in rather than absolute rules you have to live by. Then I caught the end of a TV documentary presented by Stephen Fry or Richard Dawkins and whichever one it was said: 'We shouldn't believe in something just because it feels right,' just because it fits.

At university, I was given a leaflet by the Christian society with responses to common critiques of the faith. One argument was against the claim that 'faith is a psychological crutch'. I had never heard the phrase before and it stuck. The 'myth' the Christian society was trying to 'bust' stayed with me and their counterargument did not. I did tend to lean on faith to cope with an uncertain and cruel world, although also to practise gratitude and humility in light of my successes. I liked the basic tenets I'd taken from it. I still do. It was the Church as an institution that I found off-putting: the rules, the judgement, the deference to elders without justification and the hypocrisy.

In 2019, I went with my dad to the historic consecration of Reverend Rose Hudson-Wilkin, the first black woman to become a Church of England bishop. I like to see black women winning and I didn't need to be part of the Church as an institution to know what it meant. I initially sat towards the back of St Paul's Cathedral, in the same vein that you wouldn't go to the front of a crowd for a band unless you were a major fan. I've only read the Children's Bible in full, so it didn't seem fair to take front-row seats. A friendly man sitting in front of me asked me what congregation I was a part of and in a panic I said I was a Quaker. I have a lot of time for Quakers, who have a history of being on the right side of things. I went to a Quaker school. So if I was going to pick a type of Christianity, that would be it. I've defaulted to this cover story more than once.

So if someone assumes I'm a Christian I rarely correct them. While doing research for my master's thesis, I went to the Jamaican Diaspora conference in Birmingham. I took the train back to London with a trainee nurse who had recently moved to the capital. She told me she had been struggling, because her flatmates partied relentlessly, drank copiously and were essentially morally degenerate. She had found solace in her church, which she tried to encourage me to attend a number of times throughout the journey. I felt for her, as a good flat share is a place shared with like-minded people. But I didn't have the heart to tell her I had a lot more in common with the flatmates who terrified her. As the conversation and the train trotted on, I said, for a reason now unclear, that I didn't always listen to my parents and that respect is earned, not an automatic right. She told me you should always listen to and respect your parents, no matter what, as clearly outlined in Ephesians 6:1–2. I knew I'd never attend her church. I didn't see what any of this had to do with trying to be a good person. To me, being a good person is trying your best to act with conviction, supporting your peers as best you can, and trying to improve other people's circumstances. It's not about being perfect and certainly not about deference.

'There's this kind of irony of respectability, holiness and a kind of false naivety that we go along with in Christian spaces that we all know is crap,' Reverend Jarel Robinson-Brown, Curate at St Botolph without Aldgate Diocese in London, told me. 'We're all afraid of reality to some extent, and we're all afraid of truth. And so to have a Christian space, where we can pretend, that can be a nice refuge. So we fool ourselves for, like, an hour on a Sunday morning, thinking we're all a bit more like God than we are, and that we're all as respectable as we pretend to be.'

A sanctuary from life realities, demands and pressures, where once a week you can wear your Sunday best, and present the best versions of yourself to your community, isn't inherently bad. But it can tip into something more malign. What happens when the messiness of life doesn't match up with the image people are used to you portraying? 'When the mask slips or that particular family falls apart, or that person's unfaithful, or that person has a breakdown, the shame and guilt comes, and we still don't talk about it,' Robinson-Brown said. 'Because we're supposed to be unbreakable. Because God is faithful. And that is all to do with respectability. And it's, it's such a burden. And I do think it's a distinctly Christian problem.'

Because my engagement with the organised elements of Christianity was limited at an early age, I haven't been badly affected by this pressure. The few people I know who hold religious beliefs live them by committing to justice rather than judgement, and that shines through the work that they do. Some of the experiences a lot of black women hold have not happened to me. There's no pressure for me to date in order to marry.[10] I stopped believing that you should try and wait for marriage to have sex in my early teens, so did not go through any internal conflicts.[11] I was not subject to purity culture, that I should dress modestly even if I didn't want to, nor was I policed for supposed sexual wrongdoing.[12] I did not have to enter any discourse as to whether black Christians should go to Afro Nation or if it was a Petri dish of wayward behaviour.[13] And I didn't risk losing a close-knit community or key source of my social life by not believing or deciding to defy expectations.

'When people come to this country, the first thing they look for, is that kind of religious forum which they're used to, so that they can pick up their social life. It's not always just about the belief,' Clive Aruede, co-founder of the Association of Black Humanists (ABH), told me. 'It's about the sort of social life that you get when you are in a church or in some kind of religious environment.'

On 17 February 1961, the Labour MP Mr Fletcher is one of a small group of MPs defending West Indian migrants from the more hostile elements of Parliament. In a debate in the House of Commons titled 'Control of Immigration' where MPs' speeches are laced with racism that sadly wouldn't look out of place in the 2020s, Mr Fletcher makes it clear that these migrants aren't criminals clogging up council house waiting lists. They are good, God-fearing people and a quick visit to 'any of the well-known London churches' would show his fellow MPs, and the public, that. His parish church in Islington, in fact, has 'a very high proportion of coloured people among the congregation'.[14]

In the 1960s, an average of 69 per cent of the total population in the British Caribbean attended one of the six major branches of the Christian church regularly: Roman Catholic, Church of England, Baptist, Congregational, Methodist, and Presbyterian. Once living in Greater London, only 4 per cent of the West Indian immigrants attended these sects. Similar patterns were found in other parts of the country. It's not that their beliefs had changed, their environment had. A combination of rejection by white congregations, class difference between the mostly working-class black migrants and middle-class white Brits, and different styles of worship lent itself to black migrants building their own church communities.[15] In an interview with *Christianity Today*, Chine McDonald, the Director of the religion and society think-tank Theos (then at Christian Aid at the time of the interview), described a similar pattern for Nigerian migrants in the 1980s.[16] Rejecting Christianity, or even questioning it, can be read as a refusal of community and risks losing the support and identity it provides.

'I wrote an email [and] explained why I no longer believed, that I didn't see any evidence for any supernatural entities. I sent it off to everyone on my email list. And, of course, the phone didn't stop ringing for days,' Aruede from ABH told me. He set up the organisation with Lola Tinubu to support African and Caribbean people who have left, or are thinking of leaving, religion. After his mass email, Aruede 'even had a couple of people fly over from Nigeria, to try and persuade me and get me back into the religious fold'.

After leaving school, he took an interest in science and space and eventually started to enter online forums on atheism. 'When I first left, it was just like, you're coming off drugs or something, to suddenly let go of all those beliefs,' he said.

Tinubu, and Audrey Simmons, an organiser with ABH, both waited until their mothers had died before telling people they no longer had faith. 'You're not just saying I believe/I don't believe, you're also unpacking your life,' Simmons said. Tinubu found family, friends and even strangers took it as a personal rejection. 'I don't rely on anyone. Imagine if you have to rely on your parents, for your tuition or accommodation?'

Simmons' family are OK with her leaving the Seventh-day Adventist sect behind. They just think she's a bit weird. She's the lone, contrary voice in their family WhatsApp and relishes it. When she meets the new partner of a family member and catches the cheeky glance that says, 'She's the weird aunty,' she's fine with it. What's harder, is when a lack of belief and a lack of 'morality' are conflated. When her brother realised that her humanism wasn't a phase, that she wasn't just a teenager temporarily dabbling in hairstyles and subcultures but an adult deciding it was the way she permanently wanted to live, he began to worry. Before she went on a holiday, he held her and urged her to remember the lessons of their mother about men. 'I mean, I wasn't *not* shagging them before because of God! I'm not gonna start shagging them now because I haven't got God. It was just this idea that suddenly I was going to become some wanton tart,' she said. 'And that's what you're trying to balance. So you're having to live this life not being a tart. I might be, but I'd have to hide it. You're scrutinised just a little bit more if you do something: ah well, you know, she's an unbeliever, what do you expect?'

For Reverend Jarel Robinson-Brown, Curate at St Botolph without Aldgate Diocese, these exclusionary ideas about morality are not in line with scripture. 'The moment you look at the Jesus of history, to the Jesus of scripture, you can't make arguments against things like the ordination of women or the marriage of same-sex couples,' he said. 'It's very hard to do that when you see a Jesus, who just doesn't seem to care about those things.' In his book, *Black Gay British Christian Queer: The Church and the Famine of Grace*, he argued that the Christian community in the UK proclaims that love is for all and all are welcome in name only. In reality, people are divided into binaries: the deserving and undeserving, the good and the bad, the saint and the sinner, and included and excluded depending on which side they fall. The Church of England's role in the slave trade and colonialism and the testament of LGBTQ+ Christians are examples of this 'famine of grace', the gap between the gospel and the realities of church life. The policies and attitudes that are designed to keep certain people out.[17]

'We have to look at what Jesus does, how he lives, how he dies, how he rises again, and where he places his body. Amongst the poor, amongst the oppressed, amongst sinners. The famine of grace is what is created when people are hungry and are starved, of being in relationship with that Jesus who loves them just as they are, and he wants to be alongside them,' he told me. 'The situation in the churches, where people are allowed to say that they don't believe that women can become bishops. They don't think that gay people should be allowed to get married or that we should baptise the kids of same-sex couples.'

Attitudes to the LGBTQ+ community in Britain's former empire are rooted in Sections 76 and 77 of the Offences Against the Person Act of 1861, which were exported from Westminster to the colonies. This criminalised 'buggery' and 'gross indecency' as punishable by imprisonment and its legacy lives on. Of the seventy-two countries with such a law still on the books, over half of them, at least thirty-six, were once subject to some sort of British colonial rule.[18] The moral mission of the legislators was to impose 'Christian' values onto colonial subjects. More recently, American evangelical churches with extreme anti-LGBTQ+ views have found new audiences in Britain's former empire. Many of these countries have their own resistance movements, and although attitudes have begun to thaw slowly, discrimination and violence is still a reality for LGBTQ+ people.*

In the black British community, these homophobic attitudes live on but, over time, they have lessened. The latest iteration of the National Survey of Sexual Attitudes has been delayed by Covid-19, so we only have data from 1990–2010. Dr Laura Watt and Professor Mark Elliot's analysis saw a decline in homophobic attitudes among black and South Asian people and religious people. But homophobic attitudes were still recorded at much higher rates than among the white British majority and non-religious groups. In 1990, 67 per cent of black and South Asian sixteen-to-forty-four-year-olds believed that same-sex relationships were always wrong, a number that fell to 58 per cent by 2010. For white respondents in this age bracket, only 12 per cent held this view in 2010. Religious belief had a similar effect. In 2010, 60 per cent of sixteen-to-forty-four-year-olds who attended at least one religious service a week viewed homosexuality as always wrong, compared with only 11 per cent of those who didn't identify as religious.[19]

The perpetuation of sexism, homophobia and transphobia all contributed to my disillusionment with Christianity. It didn't chime with the values I'd interpreted from my shallow understanding of scripture, so I became uninterested in it. '[The church] is often the first place a lot of people look to, when they're looking to encounter Jesus, understandably,' Robinson-Brown told me. 'And sadly, so rarely, people find him there, they find a very different thing.'

That's what makes his own congregation sound so special. 'On a Sunday morning, I look out and think I can't see any other space

* For example, LGBT+ Rights Ghana https://www.lgbtrightsgh.org/ and JFLAG (Jamaica) https://www.equalityjamaica.org/

where all of you people, we have trans folk, we have heterosexual, black folk, young and old, children, old people, people from China, we have a brain surgeon in our church, and on a Sunday morning, these people are sitting side by side. That's not happening anywhere else in society, really.'

Although faith isn't for me, I have a profound respect for the work of Robinson-Brown and the space he and his colleagues like Jide Macaulay, an openly gay Anglican priest and founder of the House of Rainbow, are creating to build community with black LGBTQ+ Christians. A community that centres love, grace and justice.

I saw similarities in the experiences of the Black Humanists and the work of Jarel Robinson-Brown. The first was the reluctance of mainstream institutions to acknowledge the role racism and colonialism played in the formation and development of their belief systems. While Anglicans including William Wilberforce or John Newton campaigned for the abolition of the slave trade, research by University College London's Legacies of British Slave Ownership uncovered that individual clergy received payments under 1833 Abolition of Slavery Act compensating them for slaves they or their families 'owned'.[20]

In 2006, the General Synod of the Church of England voted in favour of issuing an apology for its role in the slave trade. In January 2023, the Church of England pledged £100m to "address past wrongs", after its investment fund was found to have historic links to slavery.[21] However, progress on racial justice within the institution has been slow. Dr Elizabeth Henry, the former National Adviser for Minority-Ethnic Anglican Concerns, left her position in 2020, citing 'a willingness in principle, but not in practice, to tackle racism' as an issue.[22] In an article in *Church Times*, Chine McDonald added that 'the Church remains steeped in white supremacy. By white supremacy, I mean the pervasive yet often subconscious idea that whiteness is better, or best, which finds its way into every parish in the country through monochrome church leadership.'[23] And although Christianity was established in Africa long before European colonisation, this history is missing in the theology curriculum. 'I was taught Augustine when I was studying theology, [but] no one mentioned his African-ness to me at all. No one told me that St Mark went to Africa and was martyred there in Alexandria. No one told me that,' Robinson-Brown said.

For the Black Humanists, they were met with resistance when they critiqued Enlightenment philosophers like Emmanuel Kant and Voltaire and their descriptions of Africans. There was also an unwillingness to engage with other thinkers. 'They don't know what to do with it,' Audrey Simmons told me. She emphasised that no one was calling for a ban on Kant or Voltaire, just to give some context to their views and reassure new members that this isn't what humanism is about. 'When people are coming into this space, and then they've never heard of Voltaire and they start reading and then they're like: what did you say about black people? What do you say about Africans? Why am I in this space?'

This is one of the reasons the members of the Association of Black Humanists felt they needed their own space, to explore other types of humanism from other nations such as by Indian and African philosophers. They wanted to show black people that diversity of thought is welcome and that being a humanist doesn't mean you have to give up your culture. They hold events that incorporate members' cultural practices like drinking palm wine, breaking kola nut, and cooking jerk chicken, and reading texts by black atheists.

'We have our own space to listen to our music, eat our own food, dance in our own way, express our humanism. The concept of it is universal, but the expression of it may not be universal. We're not seeking to segregate ourselves. It's just that people are encouraged when they see someone who looks like them,' Lola Tinubu told me. 'I remember the first time we met Audrey. I'm like, going crazy. Oh my God, we are black, we are atheists! Like the first time I saw Clive, it was the same thing: oh my god, guys, a Nigerian is an atheist.'

The second similarity is the world they want to build to replace the exclusionary one we've got. 'What do we want as humanists? We want a democratic process. We want protection of human rights,' Tinubu said. 'We protested about the Chibok girls. We've supported LGBT groups. We're always on the lookout for when we feel that there is injustice.' It's about justice over judgement. 'I'm free not to judge. I'm free to accept people as they are, and make determinations about them as people as opposed to who they love, or how they walk or how they dress and if they've got a tattoo or not,' Audrey Simmons said. 'And yet, somehow we need to live together.'

It reminded me of a quote by Thomas Merton that Robinson-Brown uses in his book to illustrate what he means by grace:

> 'The beginning of love is the will to let those we love be perfectly themselves, the resolution not to twist them to fit our own image. If in loving them we do not love what they are, but only their potential likeness to ourselves, then we do not love them: we only love the reflections of ourselves we find in them.'[24]

I read the quote and thought, I can't think of a better way to try and live than that.

15 Mental health memoirs: therapy

4 December 2019, King's College Hospital

Me: There's been an . . . incident at work.

Therapist: OK

Me: It's not that bad. No one's died or anything and I'm not fired. I just had to leave halfway through our strategy day.

Therapist: OK. What was the incident?

Me: OK, so we had this strategy half-day away day and as an ice-breaker we were all given a person in the office and a list of personality traits. You're a psychologist so you probably find the premise ridiculous and you would be right because it is. Anyway we . . . we got given a person in advance and we had to . . . pick the description we thought matched them best and then pick another one for how we see ourselves. I guess the idea is we would see what traits we have and how other people perceive us so we can see how we could best work together as a team.

So anyway I get my line manager and I'm messaging my friends before: like, how stupid is this, obviously I'm going to lie. There's one that I think fits but it feels harsh and it doesn't encompass her good traits so I don't want to choose it. They agreed it was a stupid activity and advised I lie.

So anyway we go round and our office manager who's organised the whole thing has me and she picks this one for me. I've got it on my phone. I'll get it out so I can read it.

Type Three – the Achiever/the Performer
The song: Travie McCoy: '*Billionaire*' featuring Bruno Mars
This song, an ode to becoming filthy rich, is very Three-ish. Type Threes want (and usually get) the external trappings of success more than the other types.
Main orientation: Focused on success, to attain validation. Being the best at what I do is a strong motivator for me and I have received a lot of recognition over the years for my accomplishments. I get a lot done and am successful in almost everything I take on. I identify strongly with what I do, because to a large degree **I think your value is based on what you accomplish and the recognition you get for it**. I always have more to do than will fit into the time available, so I often **set aside feelings and self-reflection in order to get things done**. Because there's always something to do, I find it hard to just sit and do nothing. **I get impatient with people who don't use my time well**. Sometimes I would rather just take over a project someone is completing too slowly. I like to feel and appear 'on top' of any situation. While I like to compete, I am also a good team player.

Me: Then my managers intervened and said I'm really not like that at all, particularly because they know how anxious I get before public events and stuff. But she wouldn't let it go. I told her she doesn't know me very well and my ideal scenario would be to be alone in a room doing my work but I can't and I made a choice to do a job where you have to be in public all the time. My director shut it down and we put all our personalities into clusters but then the officer manager wouldn't let it pass and brought it up AGAIN saying, 'I'm sorry, I just really think

Kim is that one' [the one she chose]. I got through the next session and I just got this dull headache and felt sick. Then when the break came I went to the toilet and cried and had to tell my director I had to go home and I slept for three hours.

Therapist: What's bad about the description your office manager chose? Lots of people would love to be seen as successful and accomplished.

Me: I work in social justice. No one wants to be driven by external validation and recognition. The assistant messaged me saying 'I think you're a good person' after. Like it's not a good thing in our sector. That isn't what should drive you.

Therapist: Why does it matter what this person in your office thinks?

Me: . . . I don't want anyone to see me that way.

[ENFORCED SILENCE]

Me: And I guess I've been taught to be deferential and polite and grateful so it felt incongruous to how I see myself and how I want to be and no one likes the person that likes attention. I've spent my whole life trying not to be that person.

Therapist: So we discussed before about you feeling like an imposter. But if you do put yourself forward it seems – and correct me if this doesn't sound or feel right – you fear you'll be unlikeable; seen as arrogant [draws flow chart].

Me: Yep, that's it. Yeah.

30 December 2019, King's College Hospital

Therapist: How are you feeling?

Me: Good. Christmas at home was really nice. I was crying about the election. I got a bullet journal. Ready for the new year and all that! I've got all the stuff you've taught me written down in a section.

Therapist: That's good.

Me: I've been doing that 'avoidance' thing with something.

Therapist: What is it?

Me: I need to send an email. I went to these drinks for a book launch and someone was asking me if I'd ever want to write a book and because I was pretty drunk I said yes. I didn't sleep that well that night because I thought I had embarrassed myself in front of important smart people. But then this guy messaged me and said his friend is an agent and is looking for non-fiction writers. So I've been writing a proposal but I can't send it.

Therapist: You're writing a book?

Me: Well I don't know, I have to write a proposal and then it might get rejected. I mean Malorie Blackman got rejected lots of times but she's actually really talented. I'm not Malorie Blackman.

Therapist: What's it about?

January 2020, King's College Hospital

Therapist: How are you feeling?

Me: Good! So something happened. I think I had a breakthrough.

Therapist: Talk me through it.

Me: OK, so I needed to send my proposal but I was doing avoidance and I had two dreams about it – one where it was bad and then one where it was OK. I kept having automatic thoughts like – what if it's rubbish and then I'm rubbish, I'm so scared of being rubbish and it was disturbing my sleep a little bit. So I made a list like you said of all the different scenarios and outcomes – best and worst case – and I realised the worst thing would be I suffer rejection but my life stays the same. That's it. Obviously I hate rejection but it's just one moment. And even if you try something new and it doesn't work out you should still be proud of trying. And I realised I've spent my whole life trying to be this perfect person who never fails at anything and doesn't get things wrong. Like if you do everything right then good things will happen for you. And it did for a lot of my life which I know is really lucky so I believed it.

I've based so much of my value in what I achieve or how people perceive me and . . . and none of it matters. I just thought – who cares?! And I can't believe I never thought of it before.

Therapist: You've done really well, Kim. Well done.

Acknowledgements

Writing an essay collection that traces the outline of my life was a process of enforced reflection. It put the major turning points, the decisions I made and the choices of others, into sharp relief. So I want to thank the people responsible for the chance encounters and off-the-cuff advice, the persistent encouragement and unintended consequences, that have made this book possible.

Mum, for teaching me how to read and write when I was three, and for everything else. Your capacity to love and care for others inspires me. bell hooks wrote that 'friendship is the place in which a great majority of us have our first glimpse of redemptive love and caring community' but I am lucky that I found that first glimpse of love at home and it has endured. Our relationship is foundational. It is where I learnt the values I try my best to embody every day.

Ophelia, for believing in my potential and giving me access to an environment where I could develop it. My English teacher Ken for giving me Oscar Wilde and Zadie Smith to read and letting me keep them.

Eshe, for encouraging me to write for the student paper, the first place I put words together and then shared them publicly. Thank you for reading my essay sample for my book proposal and cutting one thousand words, punctuating the cuts with compliments. For someone who puts so much of their personal life out there for public consumption, I've been oddly protective of the drafts of this book. You're the only person I've shared any of it with. No one (except Mum) knows me better than you do.

Jon, for suggesting that I switch my dissertation topic from a focus on France and Algeria and to research Commonwealth immigration from Jamaica to Britain instead. An off-the-cuff comment that has wildly shaped the proceeding decade of my career but also my sense of self.

The ex-friend that told me I had an interesting story to tell. We don't speak anymore and we're not a good fit for friendship, but I wouldn't have made a concerted effort to write again when I was twenty-four, and as a consequence reach out to a nascent online magazine called *gal-dem*, if not for your encouragement.

gal-dem, the platform that changed my life. That is not an overstatement. My twenties would have been a lot lonelier without it. When I had no bylines, just vibes, *gal-dem* gave me the space to try, and to build community. I organised my thoughts and processed my politics on its pages. Liv, Charlie and Leah, thank you. And Ruth Lewy at the *Guardian* Saturday magazine, for the *gal-dem* x *Guardian Weekend* takeover that helped so many of us reach new audiences.

A petty one for the petty bitches: that guy who turned down the role at the Runnymede Trust/Race on the Agenda and told me that he was the first choice, so I could infer I was the second, after I'd finished a panel on the Windrush Scandal. That job made my career – thank you for turning it down so the second in line could take the throne! So much of the research, the thinking, the opportunities to write for major publications, came from my time there.

In November 2019, I decided to go to an after-work drinks. I was in two minds about it. I wouldn't know many people. I wasn't sure if I could muster the energy needed to be 'on', the fortitude to volley thoughtful questions and answers back and forth with strangers. I did go, and if I hadn't, I wouldn't have sat down next to the man that would introduce me to my agent. Kay, thank you for seeing value in the ramble that was me trying to describe my book idea over coffee. For your ideas, edits, advocacy and friendship. I've grown so much as a writer because of you.

Ore, you are a dream editor. You understood what I wanted to say from our first meeting. This book is so much better because you guided it. Sometimes you saw my vision for it more clearly than I did. And I'm so grateful to you and Kay for giving me the space I needed after that traumatic event; never pressuring me to speed up.

To all the friends that got me through that time. Lizzy for driving over immediately. Antonia on the phone that Christmas as I wandered Reading's canals. Amelia and Annabel for circling Bermondsey Street and its surrounding areas for hour after hour after hour. Chloe for walking the parks of Peckham with me. Chowa and I sat tracing the same conversation over and over until it had no meaning. And therapist number two, for helping me realise that I don't owe anyone the stories I don't want to tell.

Thank you to all the people who gave up their time to be interviewed for this book: Professor Sam Friedman, Dr Faiza Shaheen, the foster carers that opened up to me, Annalisa Toccara for changing my perspective, Vicky Unwin, Dr João Castel-Branco Goulão, Jarel Robinson-Brown, Audrey Simmons, Lola Tinubu and Clive Aruede, and the anonymised friends.

To the women that helped me rename those friends and transform them into avatars, who shouted random names at me in the living room of an Airbnb in Madrid. Gen, Milena, Nayeli – I love you.

Endnotes

Introduction

1 Adegoke, Y. and Uviebinené, E. (2019) *Slay in Your Lane: The Black Girl Bible*, Fourth Estate, p.87.

2 McMillan Cottom, T. (2019) *Thick: And other Essays*, The New Press, p.27.

3 Owusu, K (2016), 'The struggle for a radical Black political culture', *Race & Class 59(1)*, Institute of Race Relations (interview in 1998), https://doi.org/10.1177/0306396816642979 p.15.

Chapter 2: Middle-class safari

1 BBC Two (1972) *The Black Safari*, First aired, Fri 24th Nov 1972, 21:55, https://genome.ch.bbc.co.uk/9a839b145b2e45ecaaf09b6fb8726126

2 Exley, D. (2019), *The End of Aspiration*, Policy Press, pp.164–7.

3 Joseph-Salisbury, R. (2020) Race and Racism in English Secondary Schools, Runnymede Trust, https://www.runnymedetrust.org/uploads/publications/pdfs/Runnymede%20Secondary%20Schools%20report%20FINAL.pdf

4 Olah, N. (2019) *Steal as Much as You Can*, Repeater, p.54.

5 Savage, M., et al. (2015) *Social Class in the 21st Century*, Pelican Books.

6 Savage, M., et al. (2015) *Social Class in the 21st Century*, Pelican Books, pp.95–110.

7 Olah, N. (2019) *Steal as Much as You Can*. Repeater, p.152.

8 Brook, O., O'Brien, D. and Taylor, M. (2018) 'Panic! Social Class, Taste and Inequalities in the Creative Industries, CreateLondon' in Olah, N. (2019) *Steal as Much as You Can*, Repeater, p.151. Savage, M. et al (2015) *Social Class in the 21st Century*, Pelican Books, p.116.

9 Orian Brook, Andrew Miles, Dave O'Brien and Mark Taylor (2022). Social Mobility and 'Openness' in Creative Occupations since the 1970s, British Sociological Association, https://journals.sagepub.com/doi/full/10.1177/00380385221129953

Guardian (2022). Huge decline of working-class people in the arts reflects fall in wider society, https://www.theguardian.com/culture/2022/dec/10/huge-decline-working-class-people-arts-reflects-society

10 Friedman, S. and Laurison, D. (2019) *The Class Ceiling: Why it Pays to be Privileged*, Policy Press, pp.71–86.

11 *Independent* (2018) 'Adam Boulton mocked my working-class accent, proving exactly why we need more people like me in media and politics', https://www.independent.co.uk/voices/adam-boulton-sky-news-faiza-shaheen-labour-working-classaccent-private-school-twitter-a8597206.html

Faiza Shaheen Twitter (2019) https://twitter.com/faizashaheen/status/1141312136393777152?lang=en

12 Adam Boulton Twitter (2018) https://twitter.com/adamboultonTABB/status/1054304790874914816 Boulton was tweeting about class not race.

13 For more see Hanley, L. (2017), *Respectable: Crossing the Class Divide*, Penguin Books, pp.164–180.

14 *Guardian* (2007) 'Kyle show "'human bear baiting"', https://www.theguardian.com/media/2007/sep/24/television

15 *New Statesman* (2019) 'The human bear-baiting of *The Jeremy Kyle Show*', https://www.newstatesman.com/culture/tv-radio/2019/05/human-bear-baiting-jeremy-kyle-show

16 *Independent* (2021) 'Jeremy Kyle claims he was "scapegoated" during ITV show's cancellation following death of participant', https://www.independent.co.uk/arts-entertainment/tv/news/jeremy-kyle-show-cancelled-steve-dymond-b1914231.html

17 *Evening Standard* (2022) 'Jeremy Kyle to return to TV after almost

three years off screen', https://www.standard.co.uk/news/uk/jeremy-kyle-tv-return-talktv-the-jeremy-kyle-show-steve-dymond-b991105.html

18 *Independent* (2020) 'Burping, belching and boisterous babes: How Ladette to Lady defined an era', https://www.independent.co.uk/arts-entertainment/tv/features/ladette-to-lady-itv-sexist-reality-tv-katie-price-kerry-katona-a9587611.html

19 *Independent* (2001) 'I want a meritocracy, not survival of the fittest', https://www.independent.co.uk/voices/commentators/i-want-meritocracy-not-survival-fittest-5365602.html

20 Hancox, D. (2019) *Inner City Pressure: The Story of Grime*, William Collins, pp.144–5.

21 Reuters (2021) 'Factbox: Jeff Bezos' journey from suburban garage to edge of space', https://www.reuters.com/business/aerospace-defense/jeff-bezos-journey-suburban-garage-edge-space-2021-07-20/

22 *Insider* (2018) 'Jeff Bezos' parents invested $245,573 in Amazon in 1995 — now they could be worth $30 billion', https://www.businessinsider.com/jeff-bezos-parents-jackie-mike-amazon-investment-worth-2018-7?r=US&IR=T

23 Friedman, S et al. (2021). Deflecting Privilege: Class Identity and the Intergenerational Self, *Sociology*, p.8.

24 *Elle* (2021) 'I'm a Millionaire But I Pretend that I'm Broke', https://www.elle.com/uk/life-and-culture/a37290986/millionaire-but-pretend-im-broke/

25 *Guardian* (2020) 'My dad said I wasn't black enough. At last, I know what he meant', https://www.theguardian.com/lifeandstyle/2020/apr/26/my-dad-said-i-wasnt-black-enough-at-last-i-know-what-he-meant

26 Kugblenu, A. (17 May 2022) *Shaking Her Class*, Soho Theatre

27 BBC Radio 4 (2022) *Athena Kugblenu: Magnifying Class*, https://www.bbc.co.uk/programmes/m0016pbb

28 Adegoke, Y. and Uviebinené, E. (2019) *Slay in Your Lane: The Black Girl Bible*, Fourth Estate, pp.25–6.

29 *Guardian* (2019) 'UK universities condemned for failure to tackle racism', https://www.theguardian.com/education/2019/jul/05/uk-universities-condemned-for-failure-to-tackleracism

Guardian (2016) '"Bananagate" highlights racism among Warwick students', https://www.theguardian.com/education/2016/apr/08/bananagate-highlights-racism-among-warwickstudents

30 Stevenson, J. et al (2019) 'Understanding and overcoming the challenges of targeting students from under-represented and

disadvantaged ethnic backgrounds. A report to the Office for Students', https://www.officeforstudents.org.uk/media/d21cb263-526d-401cbc74-299c748e9ecd/ethnicity-targeting-research-report.pdf

31 Royal Historical Society (2018) 'Race, Ethnicity & Equality in UK History: A Report and Resource for Change', https://royalhistsoc.org/racereport/

32 Melville, J. (2018) https://twitter.com/JamesMelville/status/1078747400523694082

Kelley, N., Khan, O. and Sharrock, S. (2017) *Racial Prejudice in Britain Today.* NatCen, http://natcen.ac.uk/media/1488132/racial-prejudice-report_v4.pdf

33 Li, Y. and Anthony Heath, A. (2016) 'Class matters: A study of minority and majority social mobility in Britain, 1982–2011', *American Journal of Sociology* 122(1): 162–200.

34 Daley, P. (1996) 'Black Africans: Students Who Stayed', pp.44–65 in *Ethnicity in the 1991 Census*, vol. 2, *The Ethnic Minority Populations of Great Britain*, edited by Ceri Peach. London: HMSO

35 Li, Y. (2017), 'Persisting Disadvantages', https://www.runnymedetrust.org/uploads/publications/pdfs/Race%20and%20Class%20PostBrexit%20Perspectives%20report%20v5.pdf

36 Zuccotti, C.V. (2015) 'Do Parents Matter? Revisiting Ethnic Penalties in Occupation among Second Generation Ethnic Minorities in England and Wales', *Sociology*, Vol. 49 (2): 23

37 Di Stasio, V. and Heath, A., 'Are employers in Britain discriminating against ethnic minorities?', http://csi.nuff.ox.ac.uk/wp-content/uploads/2019/01/Are-employers-in-Britaindiscriminating-against-ethnic-minorities_final.pdf

38 Khan, S. (2011) *Privilege: The Making of an Adolescent Elite at St. Paul's School*, Princeton University Press.

Savage, M., et al. (2015) *Social Class in the 21st Century*, Pelican Books, p.324.

39 Brave, R. (2022) https://twitter.com/RichieBrave/status/1523768310386814977

40 Fawcett Society and The Runnymede Trust (2022) *Broken Ladders: the myth of meritocracy for women of colour in the workplace*, p.52.

41 Ibid. p.44.

42 *Guardian* (2019) 'Balfron 2.0: how Goldfinger's utopian tower became luxury flats', https://www.theguardian.com/cities/2019/sep/19/balfron-20-how-goldfingers-utopian-tower-became-luxury-flats

43 *Dezeen* (2019) 'We couldn't stop Balfron Tower from being privatised. In fact we probably helped it along', https://www.dezeen.com/2019/05/03/balfron-tower-brutalist-renovation-gentrification-owen-hatherley-opinion/
44 Sugar, A. (2019) https://twitter.com/Lord_Sugar/status/1118127027364728832
45 Sugar, A. (2017) https://twitter.com/Lord_Sugar/status/871473813824917504
46 Savage, M., et al. (2015) *Social Class in the 21st Century*, Pelican Books, p.173.
47 Friedman, S., et al (2021) 'Deflecting Privilege: Class Identity and the Intergenerational Self', *Sociology*, p.2.
48 Savage, M., et al. (2015) *Social Class in the 21st Century*, Pelican Books, p.173.
49 *New Statesman* (2022) 'A quarter of Britons paid £100,000 or more identify as "working class"', https://www.newstatesman.com/society/2022/04/a-quarter-of-britons-paid-100000-or-more-identify-as-working-class
50 Exley, D. (2019) 'The UK's "culture of aspiration", and how the political class misunderstand it', in *IPPR Progressive Review 26:2*, pp.185–6.
51 *Guardian* (2021) 'Exclusion rates five times higher for black Caribbean pupils in parts of England', https://www.theguardian.com/education/2021/mar/24/exclusion-rates-black-caribbean-pupils-england

Guardian (2021) 'Black youth unemployment rate of 40% similar to time of Brixton riots, data shows', https://www.theguardian.com/society/2021/apr/11/black-youth-unemployment-rate-brixton-riots-covid

Chapter 4: The right kind of family

1 Chan, J. (2022) *The School for Good Mothers*, Penguin eBook, pp.26–30.
2 Peters, T. (2021) *Detransition, Baby*, Serpent's Tail, p.110.
3 McMillan Cottom, T. (2021) *Essaying*, Substack.
4 LC1201EW – Household composition by ethnic group of Household Reference Person (HRP), https://www.nomisweb.co.uk/census/2011/LC1201EW/view/2092957703?rows=c_hhchuk11&cols=c_ethhuk11

5 Garnham, A. (2019) SOCIAL SECURITY – Where have we been and where are we going? If universal credit is the answer, what on earth was the question? https://cpag.org.uk/sites/default/files/files/policypost/Social%20security%20%E2%80%93%20where%20have%20we%20been%20and%20where%20are%20we%20going.pdf

6 McKee, L. and Cunningham Burley, S. (2005) *Families in Society: Boundaries and relationships*, Policy Press, pp.9–13.

7 NatCen (2021) 'Family life: Attitudes to non-traditional family behaviours', *British Social Attitudes Survey 37*, https://www.bsa.natcen.ac.uk/media/39410/bsa37_family-life.pdf

8 Brathwaite, C. (2020) *I Am Not Your Baby Mother: What it's like to be a black British Mother*, Quercus, pp.2–4.

9 ONS (2022) Childbearing for women born in different years, England and Wales: 2020, https://www.ons.gov.uk/peoplepopulationandcommunity/birthsdeathsandmarriages/conceptionandfertilityrates/bulletins/childbearingforwomenbornindifferentyearsenglandandwales/2020

10 *New Statesman* (2021) 'Chart of the Day: The UK has the third-highest childcare costs in the developed world', https://www.newstatesman.com/chart-of-the-day/2021/09/how-the-uk-has-the-third-most-expensive-childcare-in-the-developed-world

11 *The Times* (2022) 'Held back: the mothers who can't afford to return to work', https://www.thetimes.co.uk/article/held-back-the-mothers-who-cant-afford-to-return-to-work-r5r3k9bxl

12 The Care Collective (2020) *The Care Manifesto*, Verso, p.19.

13 *Paris Review* (2018) 'The Child Thing: An Interview with Sheila Heti', https://www.theparisreview.org/blog/2018/04/26/the-child-thing-an-interview-with-sheila-heti/Cosslett, R.L. (2022) https://twitter.com/rhiannonlucyc/status/1564319739379425285

14 @OohEddie Twitter account, https://twitter.com/OohEddie/status/1048562319331143682 David Lammy MP (2018) https://twitter.com/DavidLammy/status/1048882522782932994

15 White, N. (2018) 'More offensive statements found in GCSE textbook pulled from shelves amid charges of racism', https://www.huffingtonpost.co.uk/entry/offensive-statements-gcse-textbook_uk_5bc4af5ce4b0bd9ed55c8325

16 BBC News (2018) 'GCSE book pulled after stereotyping Caribbean dads as "largely absent"' https://www.bbc.co.uk/news/newsbeat-45784222

17 Ibid.

18 For example, Jean-Louis Flandrin argues it started to take recognisable shape in the nineteenth century. But that outside of the aristocracy, the concept of the family unit in England is in a historical sense, a fairly recent one. Flandrin, J.F. (1976) *Families in Former Times: Kinship, Households and Sexuality*, Cambridge University Press, pp.1–10. One of the most famous critiques of the rise of the nuclear family is by Fredrich Engels in *The Origin of the Family, Private Property and the State* (1884). For an alternative perspective see Scott Smith, D. (1993) 'The Curious History of Theorizing about the History of the Western Nuclear Family', *Social Science History*, Vol. 17, No. 3 (Autumn, 1993), pp.325–53.

19 Steve Ruggles (1987) *Prolonged Connections The Rise of the Extended Family in Nineteenth-Century England and America*, University of Wisconsin Press, p.6–9.

20 The Future Laboratory (2019) 'Families have evolved. Why haven't brands caught up?', https://www.thefuturelaboratory.com/blog/families-have-evolved.-why-havent-brands-caught-up

21 Nash, C., O'Malley, L. and Patterson, M. (2018) 'A Critique of Family Representation by Marketers in Advertising', https://www.researchgate.net/publication/327601746_A_Critique_of_Family_Representation_by_Marketers_in_Advertising

22 Barrett, M. and McIntosh, M. (2015) *The Anti-Social Family*, Verso, p.39.

23 Bryan, B., Dadzie, S. and Scafe, S. (2018) *Heart of the Race: Black Women's Lives in Britain*, Verso, p.213.

24 Lord Moyne (1938) *West India Royal commission report* https://www.bl.uk/collection-items/the-moyne-report

25 Mohammed, P. and Shepherd, C., eds.(1999), 'Gender in Caribbean Development. Trinidad and Tobago: University of the West Indies', *Women and Development Studies Project*. pp.156–69.

26 Reynolds, T. (2005) *Caribbean Mothers: Identity and Experience in the UK*, The Tufnell Press, p.36.

27 Rose, J. (1969) *Colour and Citizenship*, A Report on British Race Relations', Institute of Race Relations, p.48.

28 Davison (1966) *Black British: Immigrants to England*, Oxford University Press, pp.30–1.

29 Rose, J. (1969) 'Colour and Citizenship: A Report on British Race Relations', Institute of Race Relations, p.48.

30 Davison, R.B. (1966) *Black British: Immigrants to England*, Oxford University Press, p.144–7. Maunder, W.F. (1955) 'The New Jamaican

Emigration', *Social and Economic Studies* 4, pp.45–6.

31 *Guardian* (2010) 'Black boys are too feminised', https://www.theguardian.com/commentisfree/2010/mar/15/black-boys-too-feminised-fathers

32 *Guardian* (2021) 'The UK government's race report is so shoddy, it falls to pieces under scrutiny', https://www.theguardian.com/commentisfree/2021/apr/16/government-race-report-evidence

33 Reynolds, T. (2005) *Caribbean Mothers: Identity and Experience in the UK*, The Tufnell Press, p.145–7.

34 Reynolds, T. (2009) 'Exploring the Absent/Present Dilemma: Black Fathers, Family Relationships, and Social Capital in Britain', *The Annals of the American Academy of Political and Social Science, Vol. 624: Fathering across Diversity and Adversity: International Perspectives and Policy Interventions*, pp17–24.

35 *Forbes* (2020) 'Meet Marvyn Harrison: Founder Of Dope Black Dads, Changing The Narrative Around Being A Black Father', https://www.forbes.com/sites/tommywilliams1/2020/03/17/meet-marvyn-harrison-founder-of-dope-black-dads-changing-the-narrative-around-being-a-black-father/

36 ONS (2022) Marriages in England and Wales: 2019, https://www.ons.gov.uk/peoplepopulationandcommunity/birthsdeathsandmarriages/marriagecohabitationandcivilpartnerships/bulletins/marriagesinenglandandwalesprovisional/2019

37 Morris, C. and Munt, S.R. (2019) 'Classed formations of shame in white, British single mothers', *Feminism & Psychology, 29* (2), pp.231–49. ISSN 0959-3535, https://sro.sussex.ac.uk/id/eprint/75251/3/Morris%2520Munt%2520Final%2520April18% 2520clean%2520copy.pdf This is also evident in other research such as Cunningham-Burley, S., Backett-Milburn, K. and Kemmer, D. 'Balancing work and family life: mothers' views' in McKee, L. and Cunningham-Burley, S. (2005) *Families in Society: Boundaries and relationships*, Policy Press, p.26.

38 Morris, C. and Munt, S.R., 'Classed formations of shame in white, British single mothers', Feminism & Psychology, 29(2), 231–249. https://doi.org/10.1177/0959353518787847 p.23.

39 ONS (2021) *Families and households*, https://www.ons.gov.uk/peoplepopulationandcommunity/birthsdeathsandmarriages/families/datasets/familiesandhouseholdsfamiliesandhouseholds

40 WBG (2020) 'Gender, Work and Care: Explaining Gender Inequality Across the UK', https://wbg.org.uk/wp-content/uploads/2020/04/Accompanying-paper-FINAL.pdf p'1

41 *Guardian* (2020) 'Women took on bulk of childcare during British lockdown, study finds', https://www.theguardian.com/education/2020/jul/22/women-took-on-bulk-of-childcare-during-british-lockdown-study-finds
42 National Statistics (2021) Fostering in England 2020 to 2021: main findings, https://explore-education-statistics.service.gov.uk/find-statistics/children-looked-after-in-england-including-adoptions/2021
43 NAO (2019) Department of Education: Pressures on children's social care, https://www.nao.org.uk/wp-content/uploads/2019/01/Pressures-on-Childrens-Social-Care.pdf
44 Mason, W. et al. (2018) 'Social work, poverty, and child welfare interventions', *Child and Family Social Work*, p.11, https://onlinelibrary.wiley.com/doi/10.1111/cfs.12423
45 Curtis, P. (2021) *Behind Closed Doors: Why We Break Up Families – and How to Mend Them*, Apple Books, pp.216–7.
46 Metro.co.uk (2019) 'Mixed Up: 'I was adopted by two black parents – they made me who I am today', https://metro.co.uk/2019/05/15/mixed-up-i-was-adopted-by-two-black-parents-they-made-me-who-i-am-today-9535818/
47 Denton, J.A.M. (2021) The Black Care Experience, https://theblackcareexperience.wordpress.com/our-report/
48 British Association of Social Workers (2018) BASW unveils the Adoption Enquiry report and key findings, https://www.basw.co.uk/media/news/2018/jan/basw-unveils-adoption-enquiry-report-and-key-findings
49 National Statistics (2021) Fostering in England 2020 to 2021: main findings, https://explore-education-statistics.service.gov.uk/find-statistics/children-looked-after-in-england-including-adoptions/2021
50 *Guardian* (2018) 'Adoption a "runaway train often breaching rights of birth parents"', https://www.theguardian.com/society/2018/jan/18/adoption-has-become-runaway-train-social-workers-cannot-stop
51 Adoption UK, Managing contact with birth family https://www.adoptionuk.org/managing-contact-with-birth-family
52 *Guardian* (2017) 'We need to rethink adoption in the social media age, says senior judge', https://www.theguardian.com/society/2017/mar/09/we-need-to-rethink-adoption-in-the-social-media-age-says-senior-judge
53 ILO (2007) *ABC of Women Worker's Rights and Gender Equality: Second Edition*, https://www.ilo.org/gender/Informationresources/Publications/WCMS_087314/lang--en/index.htm

54 *Guardian* (2015) '"It's the breaking of a taboo": the parents who regret having children', https://www.theguardian.com/lifeandstyle/2017/feb/11/breaking-taboo-parents-who-regret-having-children
55 Lewis, S. (2021) *Full Surrogacy Now: Feminism Against Family*, Verso, p.76.
56 Capes, K. (2021) *Careless*, Orion.

Chapter 6: Is she hot or is she just blonde?

1 *Growing up with gal-dem* (2021) 'Afua Hirsch on the Power of Rejecting Assimilation', aired 1 April 2021
2 Nomisweb Official Labour Market Statistics, *KS006 – Ethnic group*, https://www.nomisweb.co.uk/census/2011/KS006/view/1946157255?cols=measures
3 McMillan Cottom, T. (2019) *Thick: And Other Essays*, The New Press, pp.41–58.
4 Whitefield-Madrano, A. (2016) *Face Value: The Hidden Ways Beauty Shapes Women's Lives*, Simon and Schuster p.21.
5 Swami, V. and Furnham, A. (2008) 'Is love really so blind?' *The Psychologist*, vol.12, pp.108–11, https://thepsychologist.bps.org.uk/volume-21/edition-2/love-really-so-blind
6 Perett, D. (2012) *In Your Face: The New Science of Human Attraction*, Palgrave Macmillan, pp.68–9.
Tovey, M. et al. (2006) 'Changing perceptions of attractiveness as observers are exposed to a different culture', *Evolution and Human Behavior 27*: 6, pp.443–56.
7 Srinivasan, A. (2021) *The Right to Sex*, Bloomsbury, p.90.
8 Alpert, A (2020). Philosophy's systemic racism, https://aeon.co/essays/racism-is-baked-into-the-structure-of-dialectical-philosophy
9 In this instance temperate refers to 'White' European people.
10 Kant, I. (1997) 'On national characters', in Eze, E.C. (ed.), *Race and the Enlightenment: A Reader*, pp.49–57.
11 Hume, D. (1889) *Essays, Moral, Political, and Literary*, Green Longmans.
12 Zack, N. (2017) *Ideas of Race in the History of Modern Philosophy*, Oxford University Press.
13 Long, E. (1774) *The History of Jamaica or, General Survey of the Antient and Modern State of that Island: with Reflections on its Situation, Settlements, Inhabitants, Climate, Products, Commerce, Laws, and Government* vol. I–III, Princeton University Press. Dwyer,

D. (2016) 'History of Jamaica or, General Survey of the Antient and Modern State of that Island', The Early Caribbean Digital Archive, Boston: Northeastern University Digital Repository Service.

14 Davis, A.Y. (2019) *Women, Race & Class*, Penguin Classics, pp.4–5.

15 Hill Collins, P. (2009) *Black Feminist Thought*, Routledge, pp.60–1, pp.143–53.

16 Brathwaite, C. (2021) *Sista Sister*, Quercus, pp.227–32.

17 Hill Collins, P. (2009) *Black Feminist Thought*, Routledge, pp.60–1, 98

18 Sobande, F. (2020) *Black Women and the Media in Britain*, Palgrave, p.43

19 ONS (2011) 2011 Census analysis: What does the 2011 Census tell us about Inter-ethnic Relationships? https://www.ons.gov.uk/peoplepopulationandcommunity/birthsdeathsandmarriages/marriagecohabitationandcivilpartnerships/articles/whatdoesthe2011censustellusaboutinterethnicrelationships/2014-07-03

20 IPSOS MORI (2020). Attitudes to race and inequality in Great Britain, https://www.ipsos.com/en-uk/attitudes-race-and-inequality-great-britain

21 Rani Jha, M. (2015) *The Global Beauty Industry: Colorism, Racism, and the National Body*, Routledge, pp.3 and 47.

22 For more see: Hamermesh, D.S. and Biddle, J.E. (1994) 'Beauty and the Labor Market', *The American Economic Review*, Vol. 84, No. 5 (Dec., 1994), pp.1174–94.

Harper, B. (2000) 'Beauty, Stature and the Labour Market: A British Cohort Study', *Oxford Bulletin Of Economics and Statistics, 62.*

23 Rani Jha, M. (2016) *The Global Beauty Industry: Colorism, Racism, and the National Body*, Routledge, p.10.

24 House of Commons Women and Equalities Committee (2020) *Body Image Survey Results: First Special Report of Session 2019–21* https://publications.parliament.uk/pa/cm5801/cmselect/cmwomeq/805/80502.htm

House of Commons Women and Equalities Committee (2021) *Changing the perfect picture: an inquiry into body image, Sixth Report of Session 2019–21.*

25 BBC Radio 1 and 1Xtra (2017) *Too Dark to Mention*, https://www.bbc.co.uk/programmes/p05nwngh

26 Dabiri, E. (2019) *Don't Touch My Hair*, Penguin, p.99.

27 *Fortunately . . . with Fi and Jane* (2021) 'Dress smart, jock smart . . . with London Hughes', https://podcasts.apple.com/us/podcast/68-

dress-smart-jock-smart-with-london-hughes/id1220808096?i=1000422634687.

28 *Refinery 29* (2021) 'COVID Has Decimated Afro Hair Salons But Black Women Are Adapting', https://www.refinery29.com/en-gb/afro-hair-routines-covid

29 VanBanter (2017) https://www.facebook.com/BlackBritishBanter/?ref=br_rs

30 *Cosmopolitan* (2021) 'How shows like *Love Island* highlight racism in dating', https://www.cosmopolitan.com/uk/reports/a30564608/racism-love-island/

31 *gal-dem* (2021) 'Is "blonde and blue eyes" just code for "white" on *Love Island*?' https://gal-dem.com/is-blonde-and-blue-eyes-just-code-for-white-on-love-island/

32 Metro.co.uk (2021) 'Why, as a Black woman, I'm turning off *Love Island* UK in favour of the US version', https://metro.co.uk/2021/07/30/why-im-turning-off-love-island-uk-in-favour-of-the-us-version-15009450/

33 *Insider* (2021) 'If you're a Black woman who's put off by how *Love Island* mishandles diversity, try *Too Hot to Handle* instead', https://www.insider.com/too-hot-to-handle-treats-black-women-better-than-love-island

34 *Black Ballad* (2022) 'Founder's Letter: Why I Finally Decided To Stop Watching *Love Island*', https://blackballad.co.uk/views-voices/founders-letter-why-i-finally-decided-to-stop-watching-love-island?listIds=5a34ef27e9e03ed8780ef43a

35 Rani Jha, M. (2016) *The Global Beauty Industry: Colorism, Racism, and the National Body*, pp.11, 73. House of Commons (2020) *Body Image Survey Results*, https://publications.parliament.uk/pa/cm5801/cmselect/cmwomeq/805/80502.htm

36 Heather Windows (2018). Perfect Me: Beauty as an Ethical Ideal, Princeton University Press

37 *Vogue* (2018) 'Why Blonde Privilege Is Real, From Barbie to the White House', https://www.vogue.com/article/claudia-rankine-john-lucas-stamped-blonde-hair-color-race-brooklyn-new-york

38 Whitefield-Madrano, A. (2016) *Face Value: The Hidden Ways Beauty Shapes Women's Lives*, Simon and Schuster p.217.

39 *New York Times* (2019) 'Why Do We All Have to Be Beautiful?', https://www.nytimes.com/2019/04/06/opinion/sunday/women-beauty.html

Chapter 7: Awkward sexual awakening: the queen of casual sex

1 McMillan Cottom, T. (2019) *Thick: And Other Essays*, The New Press, p.55.

2 Foucault, M. (1998) *The Will to Knowledge: The History of Sexuality*, Patheon Books, p.157. For a feminist critique of Foucault's conception of sex and power see Ramazanoglu, C. (ed.) *Up Against Foucault: Explorations of Some Tensions Between Foucault and Feminism.*

3 Angel, K. (2021) *Tomorrow Sex Will be Good Again: Women and Desire in the Age of Consent*, Verso, pp.67–8.

Chapter 8: Fear and loathing on a Hackney Downs mattress

1 Angel, K. (2021) *Tomorrow Sex Will Be Good Again: Women and Desire in the Age of Consent*, Verso, p.34.

2 End Violence Against Women Coalition (2019) '"Let's Talk About Sex . . ." A short report on public attitudes to sexual ethics and behavior', https://www.endviolenceagainstwomen.org.uk/wpcontent/uploads/EVAW-Short-Report-on-Sexual-Ethics-August-2019.pdf

3 Public Health England (2018) Reproductive health: what women say, https://www.gov.uk/government/publications/reproductive-health-what-women-say

Chapter 10: Twenty-four-hour party people

1 Hart, C. (2021) *Drug Use for Grown Ups: Chasing Liberty in the Land of Fear*. Penguin Press p2

2 Baldwin, J. (1986) Keynote speech, National Press Club luncheon, 10 December, https://www.c-span.org/video/?c4451069/user-clip-baldwin-drug-policy

3 brown, a (2019) *Pleasure Activism: The Politics of Feeling Good*, AK Press, p 263

4 World Health Organization, *Psychoactive substances*, https://www.who.int/substance_abuse/terminology/psychoactive_substances/

en/Nutt, D. (2020) *Drugs Without the Hot Air: Making Sense of Legal and Illegal Drugs*, UIT Cambridge, eBook, p.28.

5 BBC News (2014) 'Why do people take ayahuasca?', https://www.bbc.co.uk/news/magazine-27203322#:~:text=Ayahuasca%2C%20also%20known%20as%20yage,US%20and%20many%20other%20countries.

6 Porter, R. and Hough, M. (1996) 'The history of the "drugs problem"', *Criminal Justice Matters, Issue 1: Debating Drugs*, https://www.tandfonline.com/toc/rcjm20/24/1

7 Koram, K. (2019) *The War on Drugs and the Global Colour Line*, Pluto Press, p.13.

8 British Library (2014) 'Representations of drugs in 19th-century literature', https://www.bl.uk/romantics-and-victorians/articles/representations-of-drugs-in-19th-century-literature

9 BBC (2012) '100 years of the war on drugs', https://www.bbc.co.uk/news/magazine-16681673

10 Ibid. Esper, D. (1936) *Marihuana*, https://movieposters.ha.com/itm/movie-posters/exploitation/marihuana-roadshow-attractions-1936-trimmed-one-sheet-285-x-37-/a/7109-87357.s Loewenstein, A. (2019) *Pills, Powder, and Smoke: Inside the Bloody War on Drugs*, eBook, Scribe: UK, pp.333–4. Drug Policy Alliance, *A Brief History of the Drug War*, https://drugpolicy.org/issues/brief-history-drug-war

11 Koram, K. (2019) *The War on Drugs and the Global Colour Line*, pp.2, 13–14.

12 UN.org, *United Nations Conference for the Adoption of a Single Conventionon Narcotic Drugs 24 January – 25 March 1961, New York*, https://www.un.org/en/conferences/drug/newyork1961#:~:text=The%20United%20Nations%20Conference%20for,consumption%20through%20coordinated%20international%20intervention

13 Drug Policy Alliance, *Drug statistics*, https://drugpolicy.org/issues/drug-war-statistics

Guardian (2020) 'The Business of Drugs: inside the economics of America's longest war', https://www.theguardian.com/tv-and-radio/2020/jul/14/the-business-of-drugs-netflix-amaryllis-fox

Penal Reform International (2013) 'The unintended negative consequences of the "war on drugs"', https://www.penalreform.org/resource/unintended-negative-consequences-war-drugs-mass-criminalisation-punitive/

Health Poverty Action (2015) 'Casualties of War: How the War on Drugs is harming the world's poorest', https://www.healthpoverty

action.org/wp-content/uploads/2018/12/Casualties-of-war-report-web.pdf

Vox (2016) 'The war on drugs, explained', https://www.vox.com/2016/5/8/18089368/war-on-drugs-marijuana-cocaine-heroin-meth

14 BBC News (2018) 'University of Manchester students "ran drugs factory from dark web"', https://www.bbc.co.uk/news/uk-england-manchester-43462064

15 *Independent* (2018) 'Four Manchester University students jailed for selling drugs worth hundreds of thousands of pound over dark web', https://www.independent.co.uk/news/uk/crime/students-jailed-university-manchester-drugs-dark-web-silk-road-a8267416.html

16 Tolentino, J. (2019) *Trick Mirror: Reflections on Self-Delusion*, Random House (US edition).

17 *Guardian* (2018) 'Town v gown: is the student boom wrecking communities?', https://www.theguardian.com/education/2018/sep/23/town-v-gown-is-the-student-boom-wrecking-communities

18 BBC News (2011) 'Fake alcohol in East Midlands is "growing trade"', https://www.bbc.co.uk/news/mobile/uk-england-16179591

19 *Vice* (2013) 'Fake Ecstasy, The Warehouse Project, And Why There Needs to Be A New Approach To Drugs', https://www.vice.com/en/article/6adpba/fake-ecstasy-the-warehouse-project-and-why-there-needs-to-be-a-new-approach-to-drugs

20 BBC Radio 4 (2013) *File on 4*: 'Deadly Drugs', https://www.bbc.co.uk/programmes/b03fb8ny

21 Transform Drug Policy (2020) *How to regulate stimulants: a practical guide*, https://transformdrugs.org/publications/how-to-regulate-stimulants-a-practical-guide p.113.

22 File on 4: *Deadly Drugs*, https://www.bbc.co.uk/programmes/b03fb8ny

Nutt, D. (2020) *Drugs Without the Hot Air: Making Sense of Legal and Illegal Drugs*, UIT Cambridge, pp.88–92.

23 Transform, *How to regulate stimulants: a practical guide*, p.115.

24 Winstock, A.R. (2020) 'GDS 2020: MDMA: not just about the dose but how you divide it (or not)', Global Drug Survey, https://www.globaldrugsurvey.com/gds-2020/gds-2020-mdma-not-just-about-the-dose-but-how-you-divide-it-or-not/

25 Ibid.

26 Home Office (2019) *Drug Misuse Statistics*, https://www.gov.uk/government/statistics/drug-misuse-findings-from-the-2018-to-2019-csew

27 Nutt, D. (2020) *Drugs Without the Hot Air: Making Sense of Legal and Illegal Drugs*, UIT Cambridge, p.343.
28 *Daily Mail* (2013) 'Major clean-up at National Park beauty spot after 2,000 Thatcher Death Party ravers leave trail of destruction', www.dailymail.co.uk/news/article-2311251/Major-clean-National-Park-beauty-spot-2-000-Thatcher-Death-Party-ravers-leave-trail-destruction.html
29 *Vice* (2017) 'How Secret Garden Party Made Festivals Palatable for Posh People', https://www.vice.com/en/article/ez8npw/how-secret-garden-party-made-festivals-palatable-for-posh-people
30 *New York Times* (2021) 'How a Trinidadian Communist Invented London's Biggest Party', https://www.nytimes.com/2021/02/18/world/europe/notting-hill-carnival-claudia-jones.html
31 Chowdhury, T. (2019) 'Policing the "Black party": racialized drug policing at festivals in the UK', in Koram, K. *The War on Drugs and the Global Colour Line*, Pluto Press.
32 The Loop (2016) *Multi Agency Safety Testing (MAST)* https://wearetheloop.org/mast
33 Measham, F.C. (2019) 'Drug safety testing, disposals and dealing in an English field: Exploring the operational and behavioural outcomes of the UK's first onsite "drug checking" service', *International Journal of Drug Policy Volume 67*, May, pp.102–107, https://www.sciencedirect.com/science/article/abs/pii/S0955395918302755?via%3Dihub

The Tab (2018) '"I kept thinking I was going to die": What it's like taking N-ethylpentylone, the drug being sold as MDMA', https://thetab.com/uk/2018/09/29/i-kept-thinking-i-was-going-to-die-what-its-like-taking-n-ethylpentylone-the-drug-being-sold-as-mdma-81834
34 *Guardian* (2018) 'Testing drugs at festivals is "a lifesaver", study finds', https://www.theguardian.com/society/2018/dec/08/testing-drugs-festivals-lifesaver-study
35 Police and Crime Committee – 3 November 2016 Transcript of Item 5 – Policing and Security at Notting Hill Carnival, https://www.london.gov.uk/about-us/londonassembly/meetings/documents/b14824/Minutes%20-%20Appendix%201%20-%20Policing%20and%20Security%20at%20Notting%20Hill%20Carnival%20Thursday%2003-Nov-2016%2010.00%20P.pdf?T=9

Chowdhury, T. (2019) 'Policing the "Black party": racialized drug policing at festivals in the UK', in Koram, K. *The War on Drugs and the Global Colour Line*, Pluto Press.

36 London Assembly (2017) *Notting Hill Carnival: safer and better* https://www.london.gov.uk/sites/default/files/pcc_report_-_notting_hill_carnival_safer_and_better.pdf

37 Metropolitan Police FOI request 01.FOI.19.002980, *Arrests at the Notting Hill Carnival from 2016 to 2018*, https://www.met.police.uk/foi-ai/metropolitan-police/disclosure-2019/october-2019/arrests-notting-hill-carnival-2016-2018/

38 *Vice* (2017) 'Here's a List of Festivals That Have More Crime Than Carnival', https://www.vice.com/en/article/zmmy89/proof-carnival-has-less-crime-than-the-uks-other-big-summer-events

39 BBC News (2019) 'Ten charts on the rise of knife crime in England and Wales', https://www.bbc.co.uk/news/uk-42749089

40 *HuffPost* (2017) 'Stormzy Slams Met Police For Linking Drugs And Gang Raids To Notting Hill Carnival' https://www.huffingtonpost.co.uk/entry/stormzy-slams-police_uk_599c04b5e4b0771ecb070a06

41 *Esquire* (2017) 'Stormzy Accuses The Met Police Of Racism After Baffling Notting Hill Drug Tweet', https://www.esquire.com/uk/culture/news/a16832/stormzy-drugs-tweet/

42 Shiner, M. et al. (2018) 'The Colour of Injustice: "Race", drugs and law enforcement in England and Wales', https://www.release.org.uk/sites/default/files/pdf/publications/The%20Colour%20of%20In justice.pdf

43 BBC News (2022) 'Child Q: School apologises for strip-search of black schoolgirl' https://www.bbc.com/news/uk-england-london-60873858

44 Shiner, M. et al. (2018) 'The Colour of Injustice: "Race", drugs and law enforcement in England and Wales', https://www.release.org.uk/sites/default/files/pdf/publications/The%20Colour%20of%20In justice.pdf, pp.15–16.

45 HMICFRS (2017) PEEL: Police legitimacy 2017 A national overview, https://www.justiceinspectorates.gov.uk/hmicfrs/wp-content/uploads/peel-police-legitimacy-2017-1.pdf

46 HM Government (2017) *An evaluation of the Government's Drug Strategy 2010*, https://assets.publishing.service.gov.uk/government/uploads/system/uploads/attachment_data/file/628100/Drug_Strategy_Evaluation.PDF

47 HM Government (2017) *An evaluation of the Government's Drug Strategy 2010*, p.105 Shiner, M. et al. (2018) 'The Colour of

Injustice: "Race", drugs and law enforcement in England and Wales', https://www.release.org.uk/sites/default/files/pdf/publications/The%20Colour%20of%20Injustice.pdf p.54.

48 Buxton, J. (2021) *Ending the war on drugs: policy, conflict and social inequality*, https://www.youtube.com/watch?v=0b8uKj6s4nM&ab_channel=TEDxUniversityOfManchester

49 Black, C. (2020) Review of Drugs – evidence relating to drug use, supply and effects, including current trends and future risks, UK Government, https://assets.publishing.service.gov.uk/government/uploads/system/uploads/attachment_data/file/882953/Review_of_Drugs_Evidence_Pack.pdf

50 Sky News (2019) 'Cocaine, cannabis and opium: Which politicians have used drugs and what did they take?', https://news.sky.com/story/cocaine-cannabis-and-opium-which-politicians-have-used-drugs-and-what-did-they-take-11737521

Independent (2013) 'So what if David Cameron took drugs? We all did', https://www.independent.co.uk/voices/comment/so-what-if-david-cameron-took-drugs-we-all-did-8954574.html

Guardian (2013) 'Who cares if George Osborne did, or did not, take cocaine in his youth?' https://www.theguardian.com/commentisfree/2013/oct/14/george-osborne-politics-hypocritical-miserable

Guardian (2019) 'High Tories: how the leadership candidates' drug pasts compare', https://www.theguardian.com/politics/2019/jun/09/high-tories-how-the-leadership-candidates-drug-pasts-compare

51 European Monitoring Centre for Drugs and Drug Addiction (2017) Statistical Bulletin 2017 – prevalence of drug use, https://www.emcdda.europa.eu/data/stats2017/gps_en

52 *Gal-dem* (2020) 'In Michaela Coel's *I May Destroy You*, drug use is just as complicated as the characters', https://gal-dem.com/in-michaela-coels-i-may-destroy-you-drug-use-is-just-as-complicated-as-the-characters/

53 Brave, R. Twitter (2020) https://twitter.com/RichieBrave/status/1326945544804163599 Brave, R. Twitter (2022) https://twitter.com/RichieBrave/status/1534144772138582016

54 A Child of Two Worlds, Twitter (2022) https://twitter.com/aChildOf2Worlds/status/1534172877687246848?s=20&t=bukQpW0MwH2_RPYajY44Zw Ro_Reveur,
Twitter (2022) https://twitter.com/Ro_Reveur/status/1534131499263565825?s=20&t=bukQpW0wH2_RPYajY44Zw

55 Drug Policy Alliance (2019) 'Drug Decriminalization in Portugal Learning from a Health and Human-Centered Approach', https://drugpolicy.org/sites/default/files/dpa-drug-decriminalization-portugal-health-human-centered-approach_0.pdf

56 *Guardian* (2017) 'Portugal's radical drugs policy is working. Why hasn't the world copied it?', https://www.theguardian.com/news/2017/dec/05/portugals-radical-drugs-policy-is-working-why-hasnt-the-world-copied-it

57 UNAIDS (2020) 'Decriminalization works, but too few countries are taking the bold step', https://www.unaids.org/en/resources/presscentre/featurestories/2020/march/20200303_drugs

Talking Drugs (2021) 'Drug decriminalisation across the world', https://www.talkingdrugs.org/drug-decriminalisation

International Drug Policy Consortium (2020) 'Parliament of Ghana passes historic new drug law, paving the way for a West African approach', https://idpc.net/blog/2020/04/parliament-of-ghana-passes-historic-new-drug-law-paving-the-way-for-a-west-african-approach

58 BBC News (2021) 'Malta becomes first EU nation to legalise cannabis', https://www.bbc.co.uk/news/world-europe-59660856

59 *Independent* (2021) 'Germany could legalise cannabis in new revenue boosting drug policy move', https://www.independent.co.uk/news/world/europe/germany-cannabis-legalised-drugs-b1960606.html

60 *Financial Times* (2021) 'Boris Johnson seeks to tackle middle-class drug users', https://www.ft.com/content/bfa779a1-2091-4fb8-b472-b3e8c328d759 Loewenstein, A. (2019) *Pills, Powder, and Smoke*, eBook, Scribe: UK, p.289.

61 *City A.M.* (2022) 'Sadiq Khan eyes partial drug decriminalisation trial in Lewisham, Bexley and Greenwich', https://www.cityam.com/sadiq-khan-eyes-partial-drug-decriminalisation-trial-in-three-london-boroughs/

62 Gov.uk (2021) *What is county lines exploitation?* https://www.gov.uk/government/publications/criminal-exploitation-of-children-and-vulnerable-adults-county-lines/criminal-exploitation-of-children-and-vulnerable-adults-county-lines

63 Black, C. (2020) *Independent report: Review of drugs: summary*, UK Government, https://www.gov.uk/government/publications/review-of-drugs-phase-one-report/review-of-drugs-summary#part-one---the-illicit-drugs-market

64 Turner, A., Belcher, L. and Pona, I. (2019) *Counting lives: Responding*

to children who are criminally exploited. The Children's Society, https://www.childrenssociety.org.uk/information/professionals/resources/counting-lives

65 *HuffPost* (2021) 'Revealed: Drug Gangs Are Stealing Children From Loving Families – Even In Lockdown', https://www.huffingtonpost.co.uk/entry/county-lines-child-trafficking-minority-matters_uk_6033cc03c5b673b19b6a12f5

Radio 4 (2019) *Life on the Line*: *The county lines gangs recruiting girls* https://www.bbc.co.uk/programmes/m0009b47#:~:text=File%20on%204%20hears%20the%20female%20view%20from%20the%20county,undergo%20intimate%20searches%20by%20police.

66 *Evening Standard* (2019) 'Boris Johnson's speech in full: Read the PM's Conservative Party Conference address', https://www.standard.co.uk/news/politics/boris-johnson-s-speech-read-the-pm-s-conservative-party-conference-address-in-full-a4252216.html

67 BBC News (2018) 'Conservative conference: Middle-class drug users to be targeted – Sajid Javid', https://www.bbc.co.uk/news/uk-politics-45707227 Black, C. (2020) *Independent report: Review of drugs: summary*, UK Government, https://www.gov.uk/government/publications/review-of-drugs-phase-one-report/review-of-drugs-summary#part-one---the-illicit-drugs-market

68 A., Belcher, L. and Pona, I. (2019) *Counting lives: Responding to children who are criminally exploited. The Children's Society,* pp.18–22, https://www.childrenssociety.org.uk/information/professionals/resources/counting-lives.

69 Black, C. (2020) *Independent report: Review of drugs: summary.*

70 *The Conversation* (2013) 'The true cost of cocaine', https://theconversation.com/the-true-cost-of-cocaine-11992

71 *Vice* (2021) 'People Are Getting Killed in Britain's Cannabis Farm Wars', https://www.vice.com/en/article/wx55dm/people-are-getting-killed-in-britains-cannabis-farm-wars

72 ITV News (2020) 'Could UK's new damning drug report bring about decriminalisation or is funding treatment the only way?', https://www.itv.com/news/2020-02-27/could-uk-s-new-damning-drug-report-bring-about-decriminalisation

73 Ibid

74 The Children's Society (2019) *Talking Change: Child criminal exploitation and 'County Lines'*, https://www.childrenssociety.org.uk/what-we-do/our-work/child-criminal-exploitation-and-county-lines/what-is-county-lines

75 Sixty Years On. Rachel Nolan on Colombia's Truth Commission Report, London Review of Books, Vol. 44 No. 20, 20 October 2022, https://www.lrb.co.uk/the-paper/v44/n20/rachel-nolan/sixty-years-on
76 *The Times* (2018) 'Manchester University students made £800,000 in bitcoin selling drugs on dark web', https://www.thetimes.co.uk/article/manchester-university-students-partied-across-the-world-after-selling-800-000-of-drugs-on-dark-web-37bv8rwh8
77 *The Times* (2018) 'Twelve years is "too long", say parents of drug dealer', https://www.thetimes.co.uk/article/twelve-years-is-too-long-for-our-drug-gang-son-say-parents-of-james-roden-manchester-university-bitcoin-7qrvn7rv2
78 *Guardian* (2018) 'Manchester students jailed for selling £800k of drugs on dark web', https://www.theguardian.com/uk-news/2018/mar/21/manchester-students-jailed-selling-800k-drugs-dark-web
Independent (2018) 'Four Manchester University students jailed for selling drugs worth hundreds of thousands of pound over dark web', https://www.independent.co.uk/news/uk/crime/students-jailed-university-manchester-drugs-dark-web-silk-road-a8267416.html
79 EMCDDA (2017) *Drugs and the darknet: Perspectives for enforcement, research and policy*, p.25, www.emcdda.europa.eu/system/files/publications/6585/TD0417834ENN.pdf
80 Black, C. (2020) *Independent report: Review of drugs: summary.*
81 BMJ (2020) *Drug deaths: England and Wales see highest number since records began*: https://doi.org/10.1136/bmj.m3988
82 Black, C. *Independent report: Review of drugs: summary*
83 Novara Media (2021) *Downstream: Why All Drugs Should Be Decriminalised w/ David Nutt*, https://podfollow.com/novaramedia/episode/22b923d35898ea5e7614e70f559d46da70faae0f/view

Chapter 11: A guide to drug taking

1 *Guardian* (2015) 'The man who exposed the lie of the war on drugs', https://www.theguardian.com/books/2015/dec/26/man-who-exposed-lie-war-on-drugs-roberto-saviano-ed-vulliamy
2 https://wearetheloop.org/campaigns
https://www.talktofrank.com/

Chapter 12: But you have Beyoncé! On race and friendship

1 Hooks, b (2001) *All About Love: New Visions*, William Morrow, p134

2 Insecure (2020) Season four, episode nine, first aired 7 June 2020, https://www.hbo.com/insecure/season-4/9-lowkey-trying

3 Esther Perel, Where Should We Begin? with Esther Perel. Friendship – My Reliable Gift, 4 November 2021

4 *New York Times* (2020) 'Can I Stay Friends With Someone Who Voices Racist Views?', https://www.nytimes.com/2020/08/25/magazine/can-i-stay-friends-with-someone-who-voices-racist-views.html

5 Daniel Tatum, B. (2017) *Why Are All The Black Kids Sitting Together in the Cafeteria? And Other Conversations on Race*, eBook, Hachette, pp. 273–4.

6 Ibid, pp.248–9.

7 Reynolds, T. (2007) 'Friendship Networks, Social Capital and Ethnic Identity: Researching the Perspectives of Caribbean Young People in Britain', *Journal of Youth Studies*, 10:4, 383–98, https://www.tandfonline.com/doi/abs/10.1080/13676260701381192, pp.389–90.

8 Hill Collins, P. (2009) *Black Feminist Thought*, Routledge, p.77.

9 NWO (Netherlands Organization for Scientific Research) (2012) 'Half Of Your Friends Lost In Seven Years, Social Network Study Finds', *ScienceDaily*, www.sciencedaily.com/releases/2009/05/090527111907.htm (accessed 26 September). Mollenhurst, G., Völker, B. and Flap, H. (2008) 'Social Contexts and Core Discussion Networks: Using a Choice Approach to Study Similarity in Intimate Relationships', *Social Forces*, Volume 86, Issue 3, March, pp.937–65, https://doi.org/10.1353/sof.0.0010

10 Tulin, M., Mollenhorst, G. and Völker, B. (2021) 'Whom do we lose? The case of dissimilarity in personal networks', *Social Networks 65*, pp.51–8.

11 Reynolds, T. (2007) *Friendship Networks, Social Capital and Ethnic Identity*, https://www.tandfonline.com/doi/abs/10.1080/13676260701381192, pp.387–8.

12 Plummer, D. L. et al. (2016) 'Patterns of adult cross-racial friendships: A context for understanding contemporary race relations', *Cultural diversity & ethnic minority psychology*, 22(4), pp.479–94. https://doi.org/10.1037/cdp0000079

13 NPR Code Switch (2020) *Bonus episode: 'Between Friends' from*

WNYC, https://www.npr.org/2020/01/22/798622605/bonus-episode-between-friends-from-wnyc.

14 Rankine, C. (2020) *Just Us: An American Conversation*, pp.155–7.

15 Duffy, B. et al. (2021) 'The "fault lines" in the UK's culture wars', KCL and IpsosMori, https://www.kcl.ac.uk/policy-institute/assets/fault-lines-in-the-uks-culture-wars.pdf

16 *Vogue* (2020) 'We Need To Rethink Our "Pics Or It Didn't Happen" Approach To Activism', https://www.vogue.co.uk/arts-and-lifestyle/article/performative-grief-online

17 The Roxane Gay Agenda, White Women Are Mad at Me (with Claudia Rankine), 10 November 2020: Luminary

Chapter 14: Atheism? Faith in the black community

1 NatCen (2018) 'Church of England numbers at record low', http://www.natcen.ac.uk/newsmedia/press-releases/2018/september/church-of-england-numbers-at-record-low/

2 Nomisweb Official Labour Market Statistics, *LC2201EW – Ethnic group by religion*, https://www.nomisweb.co.uk/census/2011/LC2201EW/view/2092957703?rows=c_ethpuk11&cols=c_r elpuk11

3 ONS (2022) Religion, England and Wales: Census 2021, https://www.ons.gov.uk/peoplepopulationandcommunity/culturalidentity/religion/bulletins/religionenglandandwales/census2021

4 Humanists UK (2021) 'New survey reveals how Census question leads people to tick a religious answer', https://humanists.uk/2021/03/04/new-survey-reveals-how-census-question-leads-people-to-tick-a-religious-answer/

5 Church of England (2019) Statistics for Mission 2019, https://www.churchofengland.org/sites/default/files/2020-10/2019StatisticsForMission.pdf

6 British Academy (2011) Religion and Politics among Ethnic Minorities in Britain, http://www.brin.ac.uk/religion-and-politics-among-ethnic-minorities-in-britain/

7 *Christianity Today* (2019) 'Churches Outnumber Pubs in the UK', https://www.christianitytoday.com/news/2019/may/churches-outnumber-pubs-in-uk-london-attendance-pentecostal.html

8 Brierley Consultancy (2017) 'The Missing Millennials', https://static1.squarespace.com/static/54228e0ce4b059910e19e44e/t/6102631a9a31cb462082239d/1627546396420/Missing+Millenials.pdf

9 Britannica, 'first cause: philosophy', https://www.britannica.com/topic/first-cause

10 *Refinery29* (2021) 'After Growing Up Christian, I'm Done "Dating To Marry"', https://www.refinery29.com/en-gb/dating-marriage-christian

11 *Evening Standard* (2021) 'Why Oloni is the sex guru Gen Z can't get enough of', https://www.standard.co.uk/escapist/oloni-uk-sex-expert-adviser-relationships-laid-bare-podcast-b962512.html

12 *Black Ballad* (2021) 'Purity Culture, Feminist Theology & The Sex Our Foremothers Never Got To Have', https://blackballad.co.uk/views-voices/black-feminist-theology-and-purity-culture?

13 *Black Ballad* (2019) 'Afronation, Anti-Blackness & The Black Christian Community' https://blackballad.co.uk/views-voices/afronation-anti-blackness-and-the-black-christian-community?

14 Historic Hansard (1961) HC Deb 17 February 1961 vol. 634 cc1929-2024, https://api.parliament.uk/historic-hansard/commons/1961/feb/17/control-of-immigration

15 Hill, C. (1971) 'From Church to Sect: West Indian Religious Sect Development in Britain', *Journal for the Scientific Study of Religion*, Vol. 10, No. 2, pp.114–23, http://www.jstor.org/stable/1385300
Church Times (2018) 'From Tilbury to the pew and pulpit: how the Church met the Empire Windrush', https://www.churchtimes.co.uk/articles/2018/29-june/features/features/from-tilbury-to-the-pews-how-the-church-met-the-empire-windrush

16 *Christianity Today* (2019) 'African and West Indian Christians Are Changing the UK Church: How God is working through the Windrush generation and beyond', https://www.christianitytoday.com/ct/podcasts/quick-to-listen/africa-uk-christianity-anglican-pentecostal.html

17 Robinson-Brown, J. (2021) *Black Gay British Christian Queer: The Church and the Famine of Grace,* SCM Press, pp.2–4, 79.

18 BBC News (2021) 'Homosexuality: The countries where it is illegal to be gay', https://www.bbc.com/news/world-43822234

19 Watt, L. and Elliot, M. (2019) 'Homonegativity in Britain: Changing Attitudes Towards Same-Sex Relationships', *J Sex Res.* 56(9):1101–1114, https://pubmed.ncbi.nlm.nih.gov/31260341/ Manchester University (2018) Britain may be reaching 'peak acceptance' of homosexuality, https://www.manchester.ac.uk/discover/news/peak-acceptance-of-homosexuality/

20 Church of England (2020) 'The Church and the legacy of slavery',

https://www.churchofengland.org/news-and-media/news-and-statements/church-and-legacy-slavery

21 BBC (2023). Church of England announces £100m fund after slavery links, https://www.bbc.co.uk/news/uk-64228673

22 *Church Times* (2020) 'Is the Church of England racist?', https://www.churchtimes.co.uk/articles/2020/3-july/features/features/is-the-church-of-england-racist

23 Ibid

24 Robinson-Brown, J. (2021) *Black Gay British Christian Queer*, SCM Press p.28.